H. DOUGLAS KNUST

More Man Stuff – More Things a Young Man Needs to Know

"A boy speaks. A gentleman acts."

– Anonymous

Contents

Foreword   iii
Preface   vi
Acknowledgement   viii

I   Relationships & Stuff

1   BFF - A Friend to the End   3
2   It's Cool to be Kind   9
3   Beg, Borrow or...Mooch   13
4   Don't Worry, Be Happy!   17
5   Your Word Is Your Bond   21
6   Girl Talk   25

II   Manners & Stuff

7   Manners Make the Man   31
8   Sorry is the Hardest Word   34
9   Music to My Ears   39
10   Have We Met Before?   42
11   Here's a Tip   47
12   Stars and Stripes Forever   51

III   Personal Appearance & Stuff

13   Look Good, Feel Great   59
14   You Nailed It!   64
15   Put the Suds to the Duds   67
16   Know How to Fold 'em   73
17   Keep a Lid on It!   77

IV   Skills & Stuff

18   The Drive of Your Life   85
19   Spare Me!   90
20   Prevention is the Best Medicine   96
21   Mow-tivation   100
22   Do You Believe in Magic?   105

V   Leadership & Stuff

23   Dream Big (and Write it Down!)   111
24   What I Think I Think   116
25   In Giving We Receive   120
26   Teamwork Makes the Dream Work   125
27   On the Shoulders of Giants   134
28   Count on Me   141
29   One Brick at a Time   144
30   The Balancing Act   148

About the Author   153
Also by H. Douglas Knust   155

Foreword

I'm humbled that Doug asked me to compose the foreword for this book. Like it's predecessor, I found it to be chock full of solid, time-tested, and very applicable advice on a wide variety of topics that almost anyone could benefit from. I can tell you that while reading the manuscript at the ripe old age of sixty-three, I was a little embarrassed as to how much of the content came as news to me. Going forward, I'll be a bit more adept at making introductions and folding clothes. Better late than never.

The author certainly knows that of which he writes. I'm especially qualified to testify to his credentials regarding friendship, as I've been the beneficiary of his for fifty years. We met as high school freshmen, when he was driving the old Mercury station wagon you'll soon read about, and we played football for the incomparable Coach Mike Dacy, whom you'll also meet through this book. Over the years, Doug has proven to be the epitome of a good friend. He's celebrated my successes and mourned my losses. He has propped me up at times, encouraged me in others, and chastised me when I had it coming. He's one of those friends who make me feel a little bit improved with each encounter. I suspect my life may have been quite a bit different had God not seen fit to cross our paths. I know it would have been emptier.

Mentorship is another of Doug's strong suits. An obvious

example is his development and history with the Explorers Club described later in these pages. I suspect one could easily locate scores of men in his small hometown of Chamberlain, South Dakota, who would be happy to recount the ways in which Doug provided them guidance and support, and confirm that he made a tangible difference in their lives. Some of these young men came from broken homes where no father figure was present, and would tell you that Doug helped to fill that void. His mentoring also came in the forms of coaching youth sports teams, teaching religious classes, announcing local athletic events, and serving on countless charitable organizations. He's always there when his community needs him. That's just Doug. Being Doug.

Leadership is another of his attributes, as evidenced by his entrepreneurial successes, and his positions on a variety of boards and committees. He's not the type of leader who merely elbows his way in and takes over. Rather, he's one who listens, does his homework, treats people with respect, and before long, it becomes obvious to everyone in the room that this is the guy they should be listening to.

As for how to approach girls, change oil, trim toenails, and honor our flag, I must assume he just took it upon himself to research those things because he's wise enough to understand that, in ways both large and small, they impact our lives, along with those of the people around us. Doug has always been interested in discovering better ways of doing things. When we were kids fishing the banks of the mighty Missouri River, he picked up a copy of the best-seller "Lunkers Love Nightcrawlers", which became our fishing bible and helped us become more efficient at landing bigger walleye. Had it been left to me, we'd have just continued putting minnows on our hooks and catching the little ones. After college, when we were both interviewing for jobs in Omaha, it was Doug who brought home "Dress For Success" in order to bring us up to speed on business attire, to ensure the best possible presentation. Whenever he takes an interest in something, be it playing guitar, sailing, hunting, preparing wild game, you name it, he jumps in with both feet, immerses himself in research, and becomes impressively proficient at it. He's the rare type of person who actually reads directions, and then follows them. That probably makes him sound like a nerd, but I'll assure you that's not the case. Doug's the guy you want next to you on a long afternoon of pheasant hunting, pushing yourself on a hundred-mile bicycle ride over Teton Pass, watching a sporting event of any type, or praying for your wife when she's battling cancer.

Masculinity seems to have come under attack as of late. What a shame it would be to allow it to become a lost art. This book can help in that regard. Most of us know a young man or two (or perhaps an older one, like me) who might benefit from the various and valuable nuggets of wisdom shared on these pages. Please consider providing them a copy. Even if they memorize but a chapter or two, it will serve them well for the rest of their lives. I'm sure you'll agree that would qualify as a remarkable return on investment.

In closing, I'll remind you to wash your face at least twice per day, look those ladies straight in the eye, and whatever else you might do, don't assume those fourteen inaugural whiskers sprouting from your upper lip will propel you to the finals of any mustache tournaments

If only someone had been kind enough to have shared those tips with me back in the day.....

Craig Kirsch

Preface

In 2001, the Explorers Club was established—a service club tailored for boys in grades 6 to 8 from the Chamberlain (South Dakota) Public School and St. Joseph's Indian School. A cornerstone of the weekly meetings is a segment I call "Man Stuff." During these sessions, we engage in discussions focused on life lessons—topics selected for their relevance to the young men and their potential impact on their journey to maturity.

In June 2020, I published *Man Stuff: Things a Young Man Needs to Know* which was a collection of some of these topics. My primary purpose in writing the book was to have something to present to the young men in 8th grade as they closed out their middle school years and moved on to high school.

I have been invited each year since organizing the Explorers Club to recognize them at their 8th grade Celebration and a book seemed like a good gift and reminder of the lessons we had discussed during their time in the club. I gave very little consideration for whether there would be a commercial market for such a book.

The response to "Man Stuff" has been profoundly humbling. From Explorers, parents, friends, and family, the outpouring of encouragement, appreciation, and book sales have been unexpectedly gratifying. The resonance extended far beyond expectations, with Amazon sales reflecting a continued demand.

Feedback from the first book has been heartening. Young men

have found practical value, utilizing it as a resource in various situations. Parents have embraced it as a catalyst for meaningful conversations, while grandparents have appreciated it as a source of shared values. The enduring appeal of traditional ideas in a rapidly evolving world is reassuring.

One of the most frequent questions I've had is "why did you call it Man Stuff? All of the information is pertinent to young ladies as well." I agree with that. Despite having two daughters, I feel confident in this presentation to young men. (But I still encourage you to buy a copy of the book for that 10-20 year old young lady you care about!)

In the preface of the inaugural volume, I hinted at the possibility of more to come. Well, here it is. I decided *More Man Stuff* was a better title than *Man Stuff 2.0*, otherwise, this book is the compilation that was foreshadowed!

So why another *Man Stuff* book? Quite simply, there are just additional topics left to cover. The topics in *More Man Stuff: More Things a Young Man Needs to Know* are no less or more important than those in the first book. The topics in the first book were easiest to write about and so they ended up in the first book. Some discussions in this volume are more intricate, leading to longer chapters, as complexity demands more detailed exploration.

Some of my critics have suggested that these topics are common sense. To them I respond "Yup, if you're lucky." Others suggest the book is too simple. It's written for young men - emphasis on young. Perhaps those critics can use it as a conversation starter and fill in where the book comes up short.

If this book can help one young man navigate the rough seas of adolescence, it's been worth the effort.

Doug Knust

Acknowledgement

I could write a whole book of acknowledgments to people who have influenced me, helped me, encouraged me, taught me or otherwise shaped me. This book would have never happened without the help and support of so many people. I do not have space here to thank all of them but I have called out a few below.

Thank you to my wife, Judy, who is so supportive of everything I do. She wears so many hats. She's my cheerleader, editor, and counselor. Her prayerful support throughout our 40 plus years together has been a constant inspiration.

Thanks to Alex Knust, my son, who designed my cover during a very busy family time after the birth of his son. His thoughtful graphics have helped build the *Man Stuff* brand.

Thank you to my daughters, Rachel Millard and Sarah Jasso, sons-in-law, Andrew Millard and Dom Jasso, and daughter-in-law, Megan Knust, for their positive support, unending ideas and input, and gentle critiques. Thanks to Megan for lending her professional photography talents to this project.

Thank you to Craig Kirsch for writing the foreword. I knew I wanted Craig to write the foreword for this book because he knew, as much as anyone, why I wrote it. He, too, is concerned about the fate of masculinity and the plight of young men. I'm grateful that my friend of over 50 years agreed to flex his writing talent for this book.

Thanks to Jona Ohm for her editing skills, her support and

encouragement, and her professional marketing skills. Jona has been integral in helping to grow the audience for *Man Stuff: Things a young Man Needs to Know* and to help me build the *Man Stuff* brand. If you, your business, your book, or some other product or service could use a boost, give Jona a call at Middle America Communication Solutions. You'll be glad you did.

Thank you to the Explorers, current and past. I continue to look forward to the Explorers meetings each Thursday during the school year. It is my privilege to work with these young men and I am so proud of their work in the community. I am learning from them constantly. They continue to inspire me with their enduring energy and optimism.

Thank you to the many friends God has blessed me with. Your example was invaluable in writing the first chapter and your influence is prominent throughout the book.

Thank you to everyone who bought *Man Stuff: Things a Young Man Needs to Know*. Your reviews, comments, critiques, feedback and ideas were helpful and priceless in writing this book.

I

Relationships & Stuff

1

BFF - A Friend to the End

I have a couple of friends from kindergarten. I'm not just talking about guys I trade Christmas cards with or text occasionally (though I do both with these guys). I spend a week golfing with these guys EVERY year. That group includes a couple of friends from college too. These are friends I am fortunate to have had for 40-55 years.

Think about that for just a minute. Do you have friends from kindergarten? How many *true friends* do you have from that period of your life? I'll check back with you in 45 years!

There's a trick to this and it's pretty simple - in order to have good friends, you must be a good friend. I know, easier said than done. But if you want to maintain a long-lasting, deep friendship that can span distance and time - I can assure you that the benefits far outweigh the invested effort.

So here are a few tips for forging and preserving relationships that last a lifetime.

Keep 'Em Posted
Choose your confidant wisely and keep them updated. Com-

3

munication is the basis of ANY relationship - especially a friendship. You need to express your thoughts and feelings to each other. If something bothers you – let them know. If something they've done or said means a lot to you, if their words or actions make you happy - let them know. Build that solid foundation of trust and empathy through communication – the more, the better. It's hard to over-communicate, perhaps it's possible, but frankly it's rare. Time and space may cause you to question if something is worth sharing – share it anyway. In life, sometimes a lot happens in a short time and sometimes very little happens over a long time – share it all.

Lend an Ear

A famous American poet, Maya Angelou said, "I've learned that people will forget what you said, people will forget what you did, but people will never forget how you made them feel."

If you want your friend know you care – to feel valued – spend more time listening and less time talking. Listening is half of the communication equation and is critical in any relationship.

But you must do more than just listen. Remembering what your friend told you shows that you care and think about your friend often.

If your friend tells you something they feel sad about, listen closely and then follow up later. Ask if he or she is feeling better the next day. Even if your friend tells you a joke, remember it so you can refer back to when you both need a laugh together. Let your friend know that you're always paying attention.

Read 'Em Like a Book

Ever ask a friend how she's doing and get a positive response that didn't match their face? Friends see pain behind the smiles

4

and act on it.

Recognize when your friend has a serious problem, especially when he or she refuses to talk about it. Warning signs that a friend is struggling could include mood swings, constantly being tired , if they stop eating or start eating a lot more than usual or even talking about hurting themselves.

Offer to talk with him or her about it while keeping an open mind. Remind your friend how much you care for him or her. If your friend seems to get worse or talks about hurting themselves in any way, tell an adult you trust immediately.

Time is NOT on Your Side

Right now it is so easy for you to spend time with your friends, especially if they go to school with you. You see them every day! But as you get older, you will find more demands on your time. Friendships will take a little more effort. Some friendships will be worthy of the time investment while others may not. You will need to prioritize.

If your friendship is going to mature, you will have to make time for your friend. It can be a lunch meeting, a phone call or a video chat. Texting doesn't hold the same value, but is certainly better than not talking at all! There is no substitute for the meaningful, memorable conversations had by meeting face-to-face.

Make It a Laughing Matter

Humor gives life to friendships. My friends and I love to laugh about past experiences. Often they are incidents that happened when we were together. I love getting together with these friends and sharing a laugh about the "glory days."

Comedy and wit are important aspects of any friendship.

Some of the best memories come from inside jokes or moments so hilarious that your stomach and face hurt from laughing.

Humor is also a way to remind each other not to take life too seriously. It's important to be able to laugh at each other and ourselves. Make time to relax, watch a funny movie, take a road trip and just be silly. It will help get you through hard times.

When I look in the mirror these days, I like to recall one of my favorite lines from one of my favorite singer/songwriters:

"Wrinkles will only go where the smiles have been."
-Jimmy Buffet from the song "Barefoot Children"

Honesty is the Best Policy

Honesty is the basis for a trusting relationship. You must approach that honesty with your friend's feelings in mind. While a true friend will be honest when others won't, there's always a kind way to express your opinion or concern for someone's decisions.

It's also important to be honest about who you are with your friend. Friends must be honest about their personalities. If you never show someone your true self, how do you know if that friendship is real? Friends accept each other for who they are, flaws and all.

No Strings Attached

At one point or another, almost all of us wonder whether someone we've made friends with has cozied up to us for another reason – help with homework, social status, or even for your mom's cookies. True friendship, however, comes with no strings. You don't think of what your friend can do for you; rather, think of what you can do for them. Friendship means caring more about your friend's needs and interests than about your own.

I GET BY
with a little help
FROM MY FRIENDS
-john lennon

Through Thick and Thin

Friends are the glue that holds you together through both the good and bad times. Friends celebrate with you in the good times and they console you in the bad times. One of the hardest and most important things you can do for a friend is to be loyal and supportive to them when you are also struggling with your own serious challenges. Caring about someone often means balancing their needs with yours.

Celebrate your friend's accomplishments. Let him or her know how you genuinely care for his or her happiness, despite how you might feel at the time.

Bury the Hatchet

No friendship is without conflict. Disagreements will come without a doubt, so be prepared to compromise or agree to disagree. In fact, some of the best friends you can have may challenge you to think about life differently. You may disagree kindly and respect their opinion without feeling like you need to change your own. You may also learn from the disagreement.

Find a level of agreement that allows you both to be happy

with the outcome.

Wear Your Heart on Your Sleeve

It is scary to let someone see parts of your personality that no one else sees, except maybe your family. But it can be one of the most inspiring things about a good friendship. Being vulnerable with someone means you can tell them your deepest secrets, regrets, aspirations and disappointments. But you can also share your biggest laughs and be your truest, goofiest self.

It's important not to be judgmental if your friend opens up to you, either in a serious way or a silly, quirky way. Encourage them to reach out to you. Let them know that you won't take advantage of their vulnerability.

The Only Constant is Change

We all grow and change. We are never the same person from year to year. Our thoughts and opinions change as we grow older, learn new things and see new sights.

A true friendship grows with these changes, acknowledging and respecting the different paths you might take. Friendship is not effortless, but it is worth the effort when you find a lifelong friend.

2

It's Cool to be Kind

Unfortunately, middle school kids can be mean - very mean! In that environment, kindness stands out.

One time, I had a group of 6th-8th grade boys on a trip, they were going through the line to pay for lunch before walking through the buffet. One of the young men was a special needs student. He had paid for his meal but was not sure what the next step was.

There was an older young man who was truly a leader in the group who had also just finished paying for his meal and he saw that the other young man was a bit confused about where to go or what to do. He went over to the younger student, helped him get his glass and walked him back to the room where our group was eating.

He did not make a big deal out of it, but was very gentle in the way he handled the situation. I watched it all unfold. It was truly heartwarming to see such kindness from a young man of this age.

After our group was done going through the line, I stepped up to the cashier to make certain everything went well. She had seen the same thing I saw and was touched by the kindness that was on display. This restaurant hosted many students and she saw the behavior of many young people. This event, however, really stuck out to her because it was so exceptional.

"Can you believe that dress she's wearing?"
  "He's so ugly."
  "Why would anyone want to hang out with her?"
  "Don't you think he's fat?"

Comments like these—or worse—are not uncommon among children, or even with adults. We live in an age where online photos and posts can return instant and anonymous comments from total strangers and acquaintances alike. These reactions can be rude, hurtful, and even malicious.

Being kind is not difficult, but it seems that being unkind is easier. Unkindness isn't new; humans have been cruel to each other for thousands of years. But today, the ease, speed, and anonymity with which people can pass judgments and criticism onto others is unprecedented.

How would you feel?

Empathy is the ability to understand and share the feelings of another. It's important to understand that empathy is not sympathy.

When we're sympathetic, we often feel sorrow for someone else but maintain our distance (physically, mentally, and emotionally) from their feelings or experience.

Empathy is more a sense that we can truly understand, relate to, or imagine the depth of another person's emotional state or situation. It implies feeling with a person, rather than feeling sorry for a person.

Humans are naturally geared toward empathy. We can lose our empathy when we are around others who are less empathetic.

It takes courage to be kind.

- Maya Angelou

If You Cannot Say Something Nice...

You have probably heard the adage about saying nothing at all if you don't have something nice to say . This a good lesson in kindness.

It's a good habit to try to say only positive things. Try to say the sort of things that will make someone feel good rather than sad. If you have a negative opinion, try to hold your tongue.

Perhaps you can praise someone's effort rather than criticize the end result; if someone isn't very good at sports, praise them for trying or for being a good teammate.

Mind Your Manners

Good manners, such as being respectful to others, greeting people properly, and speaking to people in a polite way, are also an important part of being kind to others. Surely, you know how to be polite. Do you have the discipline to do it? (See *Manners Make the Man* chapter in this book.)

Start With Those Near You

It may be easiest to be kind to those around you – friends and family. Kindness is contagious. If you don't believe that, try being unkind to someone who is showing you kindness. I think you'll find it is difficult. When you're kind to others, it will be difficult for them to be unkind to you.

You probably know people who are not normally bullies, but easily join in when others are being mean. See if you can get them to do the same when you set an example of kindness.

If it Feels Good

When you act with kindness, you will, almost certainly, feel better about yourself and the world you live in. Being kind will not only lift you and the others around you, it will also help you grow to be a happy, caring person.

3

Beg, Borrow or...Mooch

You may already know one, but if you don't, you will soon encounter a "mooch" - someone who asks for or takes things from you without paying for them. Cheapskate, tightwad, miser, skinflint, scrooge, penny pincher - all terms that essentially describe the same person: the individual who never pays their fair share.

Dealing with a friend or relative who is a freeloader can be challenging, especially if you value their friendship. You may enjoy their company, but when it comes to money or paying their dues, they always refuse to open their wallet.

We're all familiar with this type: when you order pizza, they conveniently "forget" to mention they don't have money until it arrives. They never offer to drive or contribute gas money. They're always asking to borrow money without ever repaying it. They conveniently "forget" their wallet at home every time you go out to dinner, "lose" anything you lend them, and somehow manage to escape their share of chores.

There's a delicate balance between honestly expressing your feelings about this behavior and alienating the person. So how can we protect ourselves from these financial vampires? Here are some strategies for dealing with a "mooch."

Mention their "forgetfulness" in a lighthearted way

If your friend, the mooch, frequently "forgets" their wallet, assume they'll do the same the next time you go out for a meal. Before leaving for the restaurant, you can jokingly ask, "Are you sure you've got your wallet this time?" Maintain a cheerful attitude - hopefully, the moocher will realize you're onto them, although that's not always enough to make them stop.

Communicate expectations ahead of time

Establish the rules before going out, ordering food, or engaging in any activity that involves expenses with the mooching friend. Make it clear to everyone involved that each person will pay for themselves. Ensure that they commit to the expense before committing to the activity. This approach helps because it plants the idea in the moocher's mind that they need to pay. It won't be too uncomfortable since you're addressing everyone, not singling out one person, even though one person is the reason it needs to be said.

Don't give in - be strong in saying "No"

Confrontations can be uncomfortable. A moocher is clever and will try to find ways to avoid paying. They might even hear your earlier advice (see above) and still attempt to have someone else foot the bill. They might claim they'll have money next week or use the old "I forgot my wallet" excuse whenever spending money is involved. It's essential to remain strong and consistent. They need to understand that you won't financially cover them anymore. Don't make any compromises in any form,

14

and this will reinforce the idea that no one will pay their way anymore.

Have a talk

If the behavior continues despite the previous steps, it's time for a serious talk. By addressing this issue, you're genuinely helping this person, as others have undoubtedly noticed their behavior. Failure to have a conversation will only enable their mooching. Don't worry about damaging the friendship. If you don't address it, the relationship won't survive. You'll either become fed up with being used or continue to be drained financially. Explain your feelings calmly and without accusation. Let them know you value their company but find their unreliable behavior when it comes to contributing their fair share unacceptable. Changing behavior takes time, so you may need to reiterate your concerns when future mooching incidents occur.

Hang out with them less, or drop the friendship

If your moocher friend shows no sign of remorse or attempt at changing his or her behavior, learn to say no when they ask you (IF they ask you) for yet another favor- a ride, a loan, a drink, etc. If you've been consistently taken advantage of, start taking responsibility for your own needs by declining and staying firm.

If you've given them a chance to change as laid out in the steps above and they haven't made an effort, then you might need to do the best thing for you and them: drop the friendship. A friend who continues to practice mooching behavior even after consistent confrontation, may not be much of a friend at all.

4

Don't Worry, Be Happy!

Would you rather spend the day with Tigger or Eeyore? You might remember them from your childhood and the Winnie the Pooh book series, a popular children's series created by A.A. Milne.

Tigger is a high-energy tiger who is always positive. He's cheerful, outgoing, competes in a friendly manner, and exudes complete confidence in himself. When introducing himself, he often emphasizes the correct spelling of his name, "T-I-double-Guh-Er," which spells "Tigger."

On the other hand, Eeyore tends to be more cynical and focuses on the negative aspects of his experiences. He's often sad and complains about his problems, but he remains a loyal friend to the other animals in the Hundred Acre Wood.

Most people would much rather spend time with Tigger and his jolly, friendly attitude than with Eeyore and the negativity that drains energy from everyone around him. Eeyore's pessimism can be exhausting!

That Inner Eeoyre

Have you ever had one of those days that brought out your inner Eeyore? A day when you felt like the world was against you? Perhaps the day started with lousy weather, followed by an argument with someone at home as you left for school. Then you discovered you received a bad grade on a test you thought you aced. Next thing you know, you find yourself tangled up in a mess you didn't even anticipate. You can come up with your own scenarios of how negative attitudes can develop in life—no need for my help here.

Negative thoughts tend to sneak up on you. To stop them, you must learn to recognize them. Here are some common sources of negativity:

- Exaggerating the importance of a negative event
- Becoming easily annoyed with yourself
- Blaming yourself for things caused by external factors
- Making a big deal out of minor issues
- Assuming that whatever happened always happens
- Avoiding activities unless you are certain you will excel
- Believing that bad things always happen and good things never do
- Struggling to tolerate mistakes, disappointment, or loss
- Giving up when faced with obstacles

How to Overcome the Pessimism

Find a Tigger

Seek out someone with a positive attitude. Find that person who embodies Tigger's lively and exuberant nature—a person who is always eager to make new friends and try new things. Some individuals have an enthusiasm for life that inspires those around them to be more adventurous and optimistic.

The most important thing in situations like this is to avoid isolation. Find someone who will uplift your spirits and whom you can talk to about whatever troubles you.

Stay Busy

Engaging in activities you enjoy can help redirect your negative thoughts. Whether it's schoolwork, sports, hobbies, or any other activity, keeping yourself occupied is key. Personally, I enjoy golfing, sailing, hunting, and bicycling. These activities keep my mind busy and help prevent negative thinking.

Practice Gratitude

Learning the art of gratitude before negative thoughts overwhelm you is crucial. Truly appreciate what you have in life and continuously reflect on it. Being spiritual in general will help you become more aware and grateful for your life.

Learn from the situation

Whether you've been hurt by harsh comments or thoughts from people around you, or experienced another form of adversity, use these situations as life lessons. For example, if you receive a bad grade in school, it's unpleasant and can make you feel bad, but it's not the end of the world. Take the opportunity to review your homework and be better prepared next time.

Find your happiness boosters

Sometimes a bowl of ice cream can be a better cure than any emotional counseling. Watch a comedy or any movie with a happy ending. Focus on good things in your life.

Any intelligent person can withstand the onslaught of negativity, and that means you. We choose to fight this battle and be winners no matter what. Negative situations and failures are unavoidable, but we can neutralize their destructive power by embracing positive thinking, a desire to understand the world around us, and a commitment to maintaining balance in life.

As our friend Tigger would say, "T-T-F-N" (Ta-Ta For Now).

5

Your Word Is Your Bond

"I would rather be accused of breaking precedents than breaking promises."
-President John F. Kennedy

Don't you hate it when people don't keep their word? Maybe you had a friend who promised to help you with your math but never did. Perhaps a buddy told you he would call you to make plans for the weekend but you didn't hear from them.

Many people are casual with their words. Consequently, promises are frequently made without any real intention of keeping them. When people don't keep their word, it can be really frustrating.

These seem like insignificant comments rather than mean-ingful promises. If we say things we don't mean, that aren't fully accurate or true, or that we don't plan to follow up on, what does it say about the value of our words in general?

Is your word your bond?

Do you do what you say you'll do?

How do you want people to think of you?

Are you unreliable?

Do you keep your promises?

What you tell others through your words is what they'll come to believe about you. If you said you are going to do something, it is important that you do it not just for the other person, but for yourself.

Be trustworthy. Be reliable. Don't say anything you don't mean or plan to follow through on.

Actions speak louder than words

A friend who continually lets you down when they promise to do something or be somewhere soon loses your trust and respect. Likewise, if we let somebody down because we don't do what we say we're going to do, we erode our trust with that person.

If you say you are going to call someone or do something, develop a system to remind yourself. Schedule it, keep a to-do list or set a reminder. Do whatever it takes to get it done. If you don't, you aren't absent-minded or "well intentioned" - you have broken a promise, and your word lacks value.

Over time, honoring your promises (no matter how small) can earn you an enviable reputation for dependability, reliability and trustworthiness. This, in turn, can help you develop and deepen your working relationships.

Why do we struggle to keep our word?

We make promises for lots of reasons, and our intentions are usually good. For example, we want to help other people, make them happy, or make something happen. But sadly, our actions don't always measure up to the promises that we make.

- We don't realize that we've made or implied a promise.
- We forget what we've said.
- We get sidetracked by other events.
- We lose enthusiasm when we realize that keeping our word is harder than we expected.
- We haven't allowed enough time, or we have a scheduling conflict.
- We lack the power to do what we've said we'd do.

You may get away with letting someone down once or twice, but going back on your promises too often has lasting consequences. Friends, family members and teammates lose trust in you. People lose respect for those who don't keep promises. While you gain trust slowly by regularly keeping your word, you lose that trust very quickly by not honoring your word.

Tips for Keeping Promises

We make promises for good reasons. Maybe we want to support our friends, help a teammate, or just help someone out. But we sometimes need help sticking to what we say.

- Be Organized. We often make promises impulsively. Stop and think before you agree to act. Clarify exactly what you're committing to. Don't say "yes" if you've got any doubt that you'll be able to keep a promise. Instead, politely decline the request.

- Be Motivated. It's much easier to keep a promise when you genuinely want to do so. Be enthusiastic, and don't let anything get in your way.
- Don't over promise. There will always be occasions when you know you can't deliver, so just be honest about it. It can be painful to turn down requests for help or to admit that you don't have the capacity or the ability to do something. But it's far better to do so than to risk giving people false hope or to be untruthful.
- Be Sincere. Sometimes, events outside our control block all of our efforts to honor our word. It's important to recognize that you have let someone down. Acknowledge your failure and apologize . People will appreciate it, be understanding, and you'll preserve your reputation.

It's better to stay silent than to commit to something you know you can't fulfill. Challenge yourself to begin becoming a person who keeps their word. It will really pay off in the end!

6

Girl Talk

I was the shortest kid in my class when I was in seventh grade. The only thing smaller than my stature was my confidence when I was in the presence of the girls in my class. I wilted when I was around them. I was so nervous being around them that the thought of talking to them made my palms sweaty.

The, I could not ever imagine that I would write a chapter of a book about how to talk to girls. Eventually, I figured out that talking to the girls was not much different than talking to the guys. Did the girls change? Or did my self-image and confidence change?

Here are some tips that will make you more interesting and more confident when talking to girls.

Smile

A smile tells someone that you are enjoying what you are doing or who you're with. Young ladies love it when you smile while talking to them. A glance and a smile show positivity. You don't want to do too much though. That can be a little creepy and cause her to think you're weird.

Eye Contact

When you look someone in the eye, you are perceived to be more powerful, warm, personable, attractive, likeable, skilled, competent, valuable, trustworthy, honest, sincere and confident. All of these qualities are generally considered to be positive.

Looking at a young lady directly, while also smiling, makes you appear more attractive to her. The most attractive face to show a woman is one with direct eye contact and an easy smile.

Ask Her About Herself

One thing everyone is an expert on is themselves. That makes it easy to talk about what they like, what kind of music they listen to, what movies or TV shows they watch. Ask open-ended questions that lead to to additional topics you can discuss (see below). Avoid questions that can be answered with a "yes" or "no."

Once you've asked her questions, listen! Actively listen! *Look her in the eyes.* Give them some feedback - nod your head or smile. Let her know you are hearing her. It is much easier to ask relevant questions and remember details to bring up later if you're actively listening.

What Else to Talk About

Use questions that begin with phrases like:

Tell me about...

What was the best part of...
How did you feel about...
What brought you to...
What's surprised you most...
How similar/different is that to/from...
Why...

After you have asked her about her, ask about topics like this:
Entertainment - Movies, TV shows, Local restaurants, Music, Books

Sports - does she like sports? what's her favorite sport? favorite teams(s)? etc.

Food – favorite restaurants, favorite dish, does she like to cook? Eat? Etc.

Work – does she have a job?, does she like it? Why or why not?

Hobbies - what are they? how did they become interested in that?

Family – parents?, siblings?

News - thoughts on current issues, local, regional, national

Travel - favorite place they've been, why?, upcoming trips, etc.

Use any combination of the above ideas. You don't want the person to feel like it is an inquisition so add your thoughts as well.

Remember that small talk is a necessary precursor to good conversation. It gets easier with practice. You can practice anytime you are around people. Small talk is also the gateway to deeper friendships and relationships.

II

Manners & Stuff

7

Manners Make the Man

The phrase "manners make the man" is an old proverb that emphasizes the virtues of good manners. It signifies that a person's behavior and social graces play crucial roles in shaping their character and overall success in life.

The term "manners" refers to how individuals conduct themselves in social situations, encompassing etiquette, politeness, and respect for others. Manners can help you in making a positive impression, establishing relationships, and gaining respect and recognition. By demonstrating courtesy, kindness, and respect, you can create a positive image of themselves and earn the trust and admiration of others.

Throughout the years, I have had numerous opportunities to work with young men. I have observed that, although good manners may not be flashy or draw attention, they are so rare in today's world that they immediately distinguish one from other young men.

When you display good manners, people will genuinely enjoy your company. Employers are more likely to place trust in a young man who possesses good manners. Young women will find you more attractive, and you will command greater respect from those around you. Good manners are a testament to a man's self-respect and self-control, qualities that apply to all aspects of life.

They serve as a reminder that treating others with kindness and respect is crucial for building strong relationships and achieving personal and professional success.

The most essential manners can vary depending on cultural and social norms, but here are some general manners that are universally important:

- Saying "please" and "thank you": Expressing gratitude and showing appreciation is a fundamental aspect of good manners.
- Using polite language: This includes using respectful language and avoiding profanity and offensive language.
- Listening attentively: Paying attention to others when they are speaking and not interrupting them is a sign of respect.
- Being punctual: Arriving on time or letting others know

if you will be late shows consideration for their time and schedules.

- Using proper table manners: This includes using utensils properly, not talking with your mouth full, and waiting for others to be served before eating.
- Respecting personal space and boundaries: Being mindful of personal space and not invading others' personal boundaries is a sign of respect.
- Offering help and assistance: Offering to help others in need is a sign of kindness and consideration.

This list does not encompass all important manners, but it serves as a starting point for some significant ones. In essence, good manners involve treating others with kindness, respect, and consideration, and ensuring that others feel comfortable and valued in social situations.

8

Sorry is the Hardest Word

Everyone messes up. Here's how to say you're sorry.

It's easy to give a bad apology, but I want to walk you through how to give a good one.

Do you recall the last time you apologized? It's crucial to reflect on this, as apologizing is a common part of life. If you can't remember the last time you did it, chances are you missed some valuable opportunities.

As a young child, you were likely taught the importance of saying sorry. Back then, it was easier to put this lesson into practice. However, as you grow older, relationships and interactions become more complex, and often both parties share some blame. Nevertheless, it's often our ego that prevents us from apologizing.

Apologies are often met with hesitation, making a genuine apology quite rare. We may worry about what others think of us, see it as admitting defeat, or fear that it may damage our reputation. However, a sincere apology has the power to bring people closer together.

There are various reasons why people hesitate to apologize.

We all want to perceive ourselves as good people, and we desire others to view us in the same light. It's easy to become defensive and fail to recognize our own mistakes. In such situations, we may shift the blame onto the other person or come up with excuses.

Apologizing is a simple process that involves a few essential steps. However, it's not just about the technique; true sincerity is the secret sauce to a successful apology.

Words Matter

- Using the actual words "I'm sorry" or "I apologize" is crucial. This clearly communicates that you are apologizing and taking responsibility. Without these words, it doesn't truly qualify as an apology.
- Ensure that the other person understands why you are apologizing. Being specific helps convey that you grasp the impact your actions had on them. If you're unsure why someone is upset with you, apologize for what you can and express your willingness to mend the relationship.
- Avoid making excuses, but offer an explanation if necessary. Sharing why you acted the way you did can provide important context. An honest and genuine explanation of your motivations can help the other person understand that your actions weren't malicious.

- Clearly communicate what steps you are taking to ensure that a similar situation won't happen again. Express your commitment to avoiding the same mistake in the future.
- Offer to repair the damage caused, whether it's replacing something you broke or spending more time with a friend who feels neglected. While this may not apply to all situations, it can help rectify the problem.
- Listen attentively to the person you have wronged. Remember, this is about their experience and emotions, not just yours.

Each component of the apology can be adjusted based on the seriousness of the situation. You don't need to explain your personal growth plan after accidentally taking your neighbor's trash can. However, it's essential to convey that you understand why, for example, expressing rage by punching a wall is unhealthy.

What NOT to do when apologizing

- Avoid making conditional apologies, such as saying "Sorry if..." or "Sorry, but..." Either you are sorry or you aren't!
- Do not blame the person you are apologizing to. If you feel owed an apology yourself, address that separately in a different conversation.
- Never downplay the other person's hurt in order to protect your ego. Statements like "It was just a joke," "I didn't mean anything by it," or "I don't know why it was such a big deal" won't help and are likely to make the other person feel worse.

When and how to apologize

- While sincerity matters more than the timing of your apology, it is acceptable to apologize more than once. If you're not ready to genuinely apologize yet, you can apologize once to clear any immediate awkwardness and later apologize when you genuinely feel contrite.
- It's helpful when the conversation begins with the apology but sincerity and empathy are more important than timing. Be prepared to listen.
- Face-to-face or phone conversations are the most effective platforms for apologies. This allows the other person to hear your voice, discern your tone, and interpret your body language. Text apologies are acceptable if that is your usual mode of communication with the person. Social media messages can work if it's someone you don't interact with in person. However, mass apologies on social media should be avoided at all costs.

When not to apologize

- Never apologize for being your authentic self. You don't have to apologize for who you are.
- You need not apologize when you haven't done anything wrong. Apologizing unnecessarily dilutes the sincerity and meaning of an apology when it is genuinely warranted.
- If you have sincerely apologized for a mistake or offense and taken appropriate steps to rectify it, repeatedly apologizing is unnecessary. It's crucial to demonstrate sincerity in your initial apology and take appropriate actions to make amends.

Remember that taking responsibility for your actions, showing empathy, and offering sincere apologies are crucial components of healthy communication and relationships. When in doubt, it's generally better to err on the side of apologizing and expressing remorse if you have caused harm or offense.

9

Music to My Ears

Compliments can be quite challenging to accept, don't you think? Many of us have been taught somewhere along the line that we shouldn't accept them, as if it's immodest or claiming credit for something we don't deserve. But that's not really the case. When someone compliments your shirt, they're not implying that you personally wove the fabric and sewed it. What they're actually appreciating is your taste or your ability to put together an outfit.

There are various reasons why people struggle with receiving compliments. One common reason is having low self-esteem, where individuals genuinely believe they don't deserve appreciation or praise because they perceive their actions as worthless. If you find yourself thinking this way when receiving a compliment, it's important to work on controlling and changing those thoughts.

Compliments can make some people feel anxious. They may not know how to react or respond in such situations, and thus feel intimidated by the moment. If you ever find yourself in the center of attention, which can be uncomfortable for certain people, it's helpful to learn how to act in those situations. Once you acquire this skill, you'll find yourself more at ease when you're in the spotlight.

It's worth noting that not all people are sincere, and some may be nice to you solely to achieve different things. However, it's essential to remember that most people are just being polite and genuinely want to make you feel good about yourself. Don't worry too much about the others.

When you accept a compliment, you're acknowledging the other person's appreciation of you and your abilities. Accepting compliments graciously demonstrates confidence in who you are and what you've accomplished. Compliments can serve as inspiration, as you're receiving a blessing from someone else.

Practice, Practice, Practice

The best way to overcome your discomfort around compliments is through practice. Develop a standard response for compliments so that when you receive one, you can respond genuinely. Practice saying, "Thank you. I really appreciate you saying that." That's all you need to say! A simple "Thank you" is almost always appropriate.

Remember to utilize other skills we've talked about in "Man Stuff." Pay attention to your body language and maintain eye contact with the person giving the compliment. Enjoy the moment and avoid appearing disinterested or disengaged.

You can share a detail if you want. Resist the urge to criticize yourself, but do acknowledge others if they assisted you in your success. You can express gratitude to everyone's effort by simply saying, "Thank you. We all gave our best."

If you're receiving an award, take it in your left hand. This leaves your right hand free to shake the giver's hand, making the interaction less awkward for you.

Perhaps the best way to learn how to respond is by observing others. Make it a habit to give one person a compliment each day. It's a great practice that brings happiness to both you and the recipient. Additionally, you can observe how they accept compliments and learn from their examples.

10

Have We Met Before?

Introductions provide an opportunity for individuals to connect, exchange information, and potentially build relationships. They serve as a way to expand personal or professional networks and meet new people who share common interests and goals.

In *Man Stuff: Things a Young Man Needs to Know*, I presented the proper way to introduce one's self. Here we'll look at the process of introducing two people you know who are not familiar with each other.

Few situations are as uncomfortable as when people don't know each other and no one takes the initiative to make introductions. Introductions help break the ice between individuals meeting for the first time, establishing a level of comfort and familiarity that makes it easier for them to interact and engage in conversation.

When introducing people to each other, you create a positive and welcoming environment. It demonstrates inclusivity and openness to meeting new people, which can encourage others to do the same.

The art of introducing people may sound easy, but it requires timing and manners. It can put everyone at ease and set the stage for a great conversation.

Who has rank?

Determining who should be introduced to whom can be the trickiest part. It's important to know that the person of lesser rank or authority should always be presented to the person of higher rank or authority. In a social setting, gender usually determines rank, with women being ranked above men, unless the man is significantly older. Age is the next determining factor, with older individuals ranking higher than younger ones. This distinction can be helpful when both individuals are of the same gender.

- Grandma is of greater seniority than your girlfriend.
- Your seventy-year-old male neighbor should be ranked higher than your fourteen-year-old cousin.
- All other things being equal, the person you've known the longest should be named first: introduce your junior friend to your senior friend.
- In a social setting, men are usually introduced to women, as a sign of respect. Gender is not a factor in business introductions, where rank is more important.
- In terms of hierarchy, your relatives hold higher rank than your friends.
- If you're introducing people of equal rank in the business world, introduce the person you know less well to the person you know better. Always say the name of the person you know better first.

What to say

When it comes to what to say during introductions, start by looking at the person you are speaking to first (the higher-ranking person) and state their name. Then, turn to the other person and "present" them as you complete the introduction. This makes the person of higher rank stand out as the more important person in the situation. Here are some examples:

- Introduce a friend to a relative. The relative has a higher rank: "Dad, I'd like you to meet my friend, Danny."
- Introduce a younger person to an older one: "Mr. Older, I'd like you to meet Max Youngster."
- Introduce a man to a woman: "Mary, this is Jeff."
- In a business setting, rank takes precedence over gender. If Mr. Bossy is a higher-ranking male than Mrs. Davis, Mr. Bossy gets the higher authority because of his business position, even though Mrs. Davis is a woman:" Mr. Bossy, may I introduce Mrs. Davis."

Use courteous language. "I'd like to introduce...," "May I

introduce...," "I'd like you to meet..." are all good options. "May I present..." is the formal version.

In more formal situations or when there's an obvious age difference, it's best to use courtesy titles and last names. For example: "Mrs. Simpson, I'd like you to meet Mr. Johnson." This allows Mrs. Simpson to invite Mr. Johnson to use her first name or not.

When introducing someone, it's often helpful to use first and last names: "Judy, this is Tom Johnson. Tom, this is Judy Simpson." If you know the person prefers a nickname, you can use it.

When speaking to adults, use their title unless they specifically request using their first name: "Mrs. Simpson, this is my nephew, Benji Bailey. Benji, this is Mrs. Simpson."

It's okay to skip last names when introducing your parents and siblings unless they have a different last name than yours. For other family members, introduce them by their full names unless they request otherwise. You can also mention the family relationship: "Uncle Mel, may I introduce Jim West. Mark, this is my great-uncle, Mel Carlson."

When introducing someone to a small group, you can name the group members first to get their attention: "Sutton, Isaac, Eric, I'd like to introduce Jack Jones. Jack, I'd like you to meet Sutton Smith, Isaac Davis, and Eric Thomas."

How to Say It

When making introductions, it's important to speak clearly. Mumbling defeats the purpose of the introduction.

Additionally, try to start a conversation by finding a topic that the two people have in common. For example: "Eric, I think you and Jake are both Los Angeles Rams fans. Jake can tell you about some of the games he has been to."

How to Introduce Yourself

Introducing yourself can be difficult and uncomfortable for many people. However, it becomes much easier if you know what to say. Introducing yourself with poise conveys confidence and opens up numerous opportunities.

When introducing yourself to someone else, keep it simple. Say something like, "Hi, I'm Ted. What's your name?" This works with or without a handshake.

BONUS TIP – Say the other person's name after they say it to imprint that name in your mind and make it easier to remember. For example, "It's nice to meet you, Sally." The more times you can say that name in the first few moments, the better your chances of remembering it.

Follow up with something about yourself and a question about the other person. For instance, "I'm from Chamberlain. Where are you from?"

To keep the conversation going, ask open-ended questions. Topics like music, food, sports, and weather are relatively easy to converse about.

A good introduction can set the stage for a great conversation, easing the discomfort when meeting a new person for the first time.

11

Here's a Tip

Tipping is a common and expected part of the dining out experience, but it extends beyond food service. Your barber, food delivery person, barista, and fishing guide are among the other service providers who prompt questions about how to calculate a tip, who to tip, when to tip, and how much to tip.

Leaving a tip is customary in various settings, including restaurants, hotels, salons, and other places within the service industry. Many professionals in the service industry, such as servers, rely heavily on tips as a significant portion of their income. Without tips, these professionals may struggle to support themselves and their families.

Unless stated otherwise, you should typically always tip your server when eating at a restaurant. If the service is poor, you can skip tipping, but first, consider the cause of your dissatisfaction with your meal. It may not be your server's fault. If the service was bad, it's still recommended to leave a 10% tip and inform the management about your experience. If the food was unsatisfactory but the service was good, don't penalize your server.

Take the time to express your appreciation if you receive great service from your server. Letting them know that their service was not just good but impeccable can brighten their day. Consider writing a brief note on the bill to explain what impressed you about their service. Better yet, call the manager over and personally commend the server for their excellent work.

Always remember to treat your server with a smile and be kind and polite. Service jobs can be stressful enough without people taking out their bad days on the server.

In some restaurants, a rule exists where the tip is automatically included for large groups. You will usually find a note on your bill or menu stating "gratuity included" or "service charge included" in such cases.

Knowing how to calculate an appropriate tip is also important to ensure that you tip the right amount in different settings. For example, many people believe that tipping 15-20% is appropriate in restaurants, while the tipping rate may vary in other service industry settings. Being able to accurately calculate the tip can save you time and money, while also ensuring that the service provider is adequately compensated.

Here are a few of the most common methods to calculate a tip:

Method 1: Move over the decimal in the bill total and then double that number. (20%)
   Example: $54.00 pretax bill; move decimal $5.40; double it $10.80 tip

Method 2: Multiply the tax of the bill by two. (15% depending on tax rate)
   Example: $54.00 pretax bill has $3.78 tax; $3.78 x2 = $7.56

Method 3: Double the pretax bill and then move the decimal over one space. (20%)
   Example: $54.00 bill pretax; double it – $108.00; move decimal over one space – $10.80

Method 4: Determine 10% of the bill and add half. (15%)
   Example: $54.00 bill pretax; 10% of bill – $5.40; add half – $5.40 + $2.70 = $8.10

If you're truly math-challenged, you can use the calculator on your smartphone. Simply multiply the pretax total by 0.15 or 0.2 and that is your tip.
   How much to tip
   Restaurant servers: 15%-20%, takeout & buffet servers 10%, (pretax – meaning deduct sales/hospitality tax)
   Pizza deliverer: $2 to $3 per pie
   Baristas: Zero to $1
   Hotel valet staff: $2 to $5

Hotel concierge: $5 or $10

Massage therapists: 15% to 20%

Hotel housekeeping: $2 to $5 per day

Hairdressers, barbers or nail technicians: 10% to 20%

Tattoo artist: 15% to 20%.

Restroom attendant: $1 to $2.

Car washer: $2 to $5.

Airport skycap or porter: $1 to $3 per bag for multiple bags; up to $5 for a single bag.

Tour guide: 15%-20% of tour's cost.

Cab driver, Lyft driver or Uber driver: 15% to 20% of fare; $2 per bag if the driver lifts luggage

Movers: tip 5% to 20% depending on quantity moved and number of movers

Being generous with your tips can pay off with even better service the next time you visit. This is particularly true for businesses you frequent. If you're concerned that someone in your party is not tipping enough, you can make up the difference. Establishing a reputation as a good tipper has its advantages, especially if you plan to return to the same establishment.

Who You Don't Have to Tip

There are certain professionals you do not have to tip, such as accountants, financial advisors, lawyers, doctors, nurses, mechanics, and plumbers. These individuals are typically compensated through fees or commissions, or their payment is included in other service charges.

It's important to note that tipping culture and etiquette can vary when traveling abroad. Some countries in Europe and Asia do not have a tipping culture. It's advisable to research tipping practices before visiting a different country.

12

Stars and Stripes Forever

I played the trumpet in high school and, on occasion, another high school trumpet player and I would be asked to play "Taps" at the funeral of a deceased veteran. "Taps" is a distinctive bugle melody that dates back to the American Civil War and was traditionally played by a military bugler. Today, it is performed at U.S. military funerals and memorials, as well as serving as a lights-out signal to soldiers at night.

During these ceremonies, we would position ourselves on opposite sides of the grave site area. One of us would start playing the song, and the other would echo it. We were hired by the local Legion club or Veteran of Foreign Wars (VFW) club, and we were each compensated with $10 for our effort. Combined with the relief from school for at least a half hour, it made for a lucrative deal.

Looking back on that experience, the money plays a minor role in my memories. What stands out to me is the raw emotion displayed by other veterans in attendance as they solemnly draped the American flag over the casket and listened to our rendition of the traditional song.

Contemplating the significance of the Stars and Stripes to these veterans, I can only imagine the flood of memories that these ceremonies bring back to them. For many, the flag serves as the symbol of those memories.

I don't recall how I spent any of that money, but I do remember witnessing the depth of emotion on the faces of those veterans as they laid one of their comrades to rest. I remember how they reverently treated the flag, which made me curious about flag protocol.

What Does the Flag Mean?

The American flag consists of thirteen horizontal stripes - seven red stripes alternating with six white ones. These stripes represent the original 13 Colonies, while the stars symbolize the 50 states of the Union. Additionally, the colors of the flag carry symbolic meaning: red symbolizes Hardiness and Valor, white symbolizes Purity and Innocence, and blue represents Vigilance, Perseverance, and Justice.

What to do During the National Anthem

The most common situation in which people are expected to pay respect to the flag is during a sports event when The Star-Spangled Banner is played or sung. However, many individuals, including adults, are unsure about proper etiquette during this time.

The appropriate action is to stand at attention and face the flag or face towards the music, placing your right hand over your heart. Men who are not in uniform should remove their hats and hold them with their right hand, positioning the hat over their left shoulder to ensure their right hand remains over their heart.

It's important to note that the guidelines differ slightly for those in uniform.These guidelines are laid out in the United

States Flag Code, which establishes rules for the display and care of the national flag. While the code is a federal law, adherence to its guidelines is not mandatory. The language used in the code includes phrases such as "should" and "custom." It does not prescribe any penalties for failing to follow the guidelines.

A controversy has arisen over the past couple of years regarding kneeling during the National Anthem at sporting events. It's crucial to recognize that our National Anthem is a salute to our flag. By kneeling, you are displaying disrespect to both the anthem and the flag.

The American flag represents home for our military personnel serving overseas. It serves as a symbol for the family and friends of every service member who has died in action on the battlefield, sometimes right beside them. The flag is draped over every military coffin that returns home and flies on the right shoulder of those in battle abroad, as well as those protecting us at home.

How Should We Treat Our Flag?
The following are rules from the United State Flag Code:

- Don't let the flag touch the ground.
- Don't fly flag upside down unless there is an emergency.
- Don't carry the flag flat, or carry things in it.
- Don't use the flag as clothing.
- Don't store the flag where it can get dirty.
- Don't use it as a cover.
- Don't fasten it or tie it back. Always allow it to fall free.
- Don't draw on, or otherwise mark the flag.
- Don't use the flag for decoration. Use bunting with the blue on top, then white, then red.
- The flag must be properly illuminated in order to be flown during the hours of darkness.
- The U.S. Flag should be flown above all other flags when flown on flag poles.
- When flags are displayed in a row, the U.S. flag goes to the observer's left. Flags of other nations are flown at same height. State and local flags are traditionally flown lower.
- When used during a marching ceremony or parade with other flags, the U.S. Flag will be to the observer's left.
- On special days, the flag may be flown at half-staff. On Memorial Day it is flown at half-staff until noon and then raised.
- When flown at half-staff, the flag should be first hoisted to the peak for an instant and then lowered to the half-staff position. The flag should again be raised to the peak before it is lowered for the day. "Half-staff" is meant to be one-half the distance between the top and bottom of the staff.
- When placed on a podium, the flag should be placed on the speaker's right on the staging area. Other flags should be placed to the left.
- When displayed either horizontally or vertically against a

wall (or other flat surface), the union (blue field of stars) should be uppermost and to the flag's own right, that is, to the observer's left.

- When the flag is used to cover a casket, it should be so placed that the union is at the head and over the left shoulder. The flag should not be lowered into the grave or allowed to touch the ground.
- Members of the armed forces and veterans who are present but not in uniform may render the military salute.
- All persons other than those present in uniform (military, police, fire, etc.) should face the flag and stand at attention with their right hand over the heart, or if applicable, remove their head covering with their right hand and hold it at the left shoulder, the hand being over the heart.
- To stow the flag, it should be folded in the traditional triangle, never wadded up.
- To dispose of a flag, it should be folded in its customary manner. Place the flag on a fire that is fairly large and of sufficient intensity to ensure complete burning of the flag. After the flag is completely consumed, the fire should then be safely extinguished and the ashes buried.
- Don't dip the U.S. Flag for any person, flag, or vessel.

III

Personal Appearance & Stuff

13

Look Good, Feel Great

Developing good health habits and maintaining proper personal hygiene are essential skills for life. It's easy to overlook these seemingly boring tasks, but they play a significant role in your overall well-being. Each personal grooming habit holds its own importance.

As your body undergoes significant changes during your pre-teen and early teen years, your personal hygiene routines must adapt accordingly. By adopting these grooming habits, you will not only take care of your physical well-being but also gain confidence. It's important to know that your body and breath are fresh, and your clothes are clean.

Here are some grooming habits you should follow:

Wash away those troubles...and smells!
Make it a daily habit to shower, and consider showering twice a day if you engage in physical activities or sports that make you sweat a lot. Sweating is a natural way for your body to detoxify. Since you tend to sweat more after reaching puberty, it's crucial to wash away the sweat and bacteria from your skin using a

mild soap. Be sure to rinse off the soap completely. Keep in mind that hot water can dry out your skin, so it's best to use warm water, and limit your hot shower time to no more than 10 minutes. As a refreshing conclusion to your shower, a burst of cold water can stimulate blood flow, boost mood, promote healthier skin and hair, and more.

Now That Makes Scents

Remember, body spray or cologne cannot replace a shower. It's a waste of money to use such products to mask body odor. After showering is the ideal time to apply fragrance. Less is more when it comes to using a pleasant fragrance. It can help you stand out from the crowd and create your unique identity. People may forget your name, but they won't forget your fragrance if you consistently use the same type of deodorant or cologne every day. Opt for a mild deodorant or cologne, and avoid applying an excessive amount to prevent overwhelming others. For a more detailed discussion on cologne, refer to the "Common Scents" chapter in *Man Stuff: Things a Young Man Needs to Know.*

Face It - You Need to Scrub

Wash your face properly twice daily - during your shower

is a great time to get one in. Removing dirt, oils, and other impurities from your pores is crucial for preventing acne. Use a face scrubber or washcloth along with a mild soap especially for faces. Your face requires specific care due to its delicate nature.

Along with wash your face twice a day. exfoliate your skin twice a week using a gentle scrub to unclog your pores. Additionally, don't forget to moisturize your lips. Trust me, as an older guy, if I had known the benefits of moisturizing when I was a teenager, I would have done it religiously. It will help you maintain a better appearance in the long run. Apply moisturizer at least once daily, preferably before going to bed. If you have oily skin, choose a moisturizer designed for oily skin but don't skip this step.

Trash the Teen Stache

Just because the hair on your upper lip is a bit darker doesn't mean it's a mustache. Growing out that faint baby hair only proves that you can't grow proper whiskers yet. Shaving stimulates hair growth, and while you may not have much facial hair at this stage, it's important to shave off any patchy or uneven growth. This will help you maintain a groomed appearance. If you do have a well-grown beard, that's great! Just remember to keep it well-maintained and avoid letting it look unkempt. (For a comprehensive discussion on facial hair, refer to the "By the Hair of My Chinny Chin Chin" chapter in *Man Stuff: Things a Young Man Needs to Know*.)

Brush 'Em, Brush 'Em, Brush 'Em

Brush your teeth at least twice daily. If you wear braces, it's necessary to brush every time you eat. Don't forget to brush your tongue. Bacteria builds up on the surface of your tongue every day, creating a plaque that can lead to oral health problems if not removed. Brushing your tongue daily helps clean out bacteria and food debris that could potentially cause bad breath, tooth decay, gum disease and other medical problems down the line. Remember to brush, floss, rinse, and repeat for a complete oral care routine.

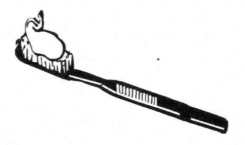

Messy Hair? Better Care

Nothing communicates "I don't care about my appearance" like unkempt hair. Take a moment to look in the mirror. A little water and a comb or brush can make a significant difference. Use hair gel in moderation, as excessive application can make your hair look greasy. Aim to have your hair trimmed at least once a month. Hair can grow half an inch per month, so even if you're growing it out, regular trims will help maintain a neat appearance. Experiment with different hairstyles to change your look. Find a good barber who can suggest a suitable haircut based on your face shape. Ask your barber for assistance with maintaining your facial hair and eyebrows if needed. Most importantly, make it a habit to visit regularly.

Don't Chew; Trim!

Well-groomed nails are an important part of your overall pre-sentation. Even though you may not think nails are significant, they contribute to the "first impression" you make, especially when you have your eye on a certain cute young lady. For a comprehensive discussion on nail trimming, refer to the "You Nailed It!" chapter in this book.

Don't Let Your Shoes Walk Off!

Stinky feet are unpleasant. If you struggle with foot odor, use foot powder to help alleviate the issue. Additionally, if your shoes start to develop an odor, place them in the freezer or let them sit in the sunshine to freshen them up.

By incorporating these grooming habits into your daily routine, you will not only improve your personal hygiene but also boost your confidence and overall well-being. Taking care of yourself physically and maintaining good hygiene are essential aspects of becoming a well-rounded young man.

14

You Nailed It!

Fingernails may not be the most glamorous topic, but that doesn't mean you should neglect them. In fact, well-groomed nails are an important part of personal hygiene. Long or dirty nails can be gross and a big turn off. Maintaining short, well-manicured nails not only enhances your appearance but also reduces the likelihood of dirt and bacteria buildup. Additionally, proper nail clipping techniques can help prevent common issues like hangnails and ingrown toenails.

The Right Tools

To achieve the best results, it's essential to have the right tools for the job. Just like a good set of hand tools, owning a set of nail care tools is crucial, with separate devices for hands and feet. Using the typical cheap drugstore clippers may turn nail grooming into an unpleasant chore. Instead, invest in quality tools that are specifically designed for the task.

You would not use a hammer for every job that requires a hand tool. Likewise, you cannot trim and care for your nails with just one tool.

At a minimum, you should have a fingernail clipper and a larger toenail clipper. Toenail clippers have longer, stronger handles and blades, providing additional cutting leverage for thicker nails. Look for clippers made from steel with high carbon content, as they maintain their sharpness for longer. While high-quality tools may seem more expensive, they are durable and won't harm your nails like cheaper alternatives that quickly become dull.

Once you've made the investment in quality tools, it's important to take care of them. Remember to disinfect your tools on a monthly basis. You can do this by soaking a small scrub brush in a bowl of 70 to 90 percent isopropyl alcohol and using it to scrub your nail clippers or scissors. Afterward, rinse the tools in hot water and dry them completely before storing them away.

How to Cut Fingernails

When it comes to cutting your fingernails, you don't need to soak them beforehand. In fact, having some firmness to the nails is preferable to prevent tearing and ragged edges. Start by giving your hands a quick rinse and brushing out any dirt from under your nails. Then, using scissors or clippers, trim the tips of your fingernails. The best approach is a flat, horizontal cut straight across the top of the nail, with small angled clips at the corners to create a slightly rounded oblong shape.

Remember to trim only the nail that extends past the tip of your finger's flesh. Avoid cutting the soft nail bed under the nail or trimming the edges of the cuticle. Any leftover corners or rough edges can be smoothed out with a fine nail file or emery board. File in one direction, avoiding sawing back and forth.

While trimming, it's important to leave your cuticles alone. Cuticles protect the nail root, so cutting or pushing them back can increase the risk of infection. After trimming, dust your hands off on a soft towel. You can moisturize your nails afterward, especially in dry air (like during the winter), as it helps keep them flexible and less prone to splitting.

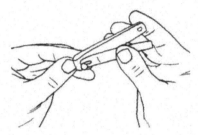

For toenails, cut straight across to reduce the chances of developing ingrown toenails. Since toenails grow more slowly than fingernails, you may find that you don't need to trim them as frequently.

Lastly, keep in mind that a good fingernail trim can be a pleasant and satisfying experience. It's hard for most guys to believe, but mani-pedi spas exist for a reason. Knowing how to care for your nails not only saves you time and money but also allows you to appreciate the expertise of professionals when you do visit a spa or barbershop.

Upgrading your nail grooming routine is a minor change in your life. It involves purchasing higher-quality tools and incorporating cleaning and filing steps into your trimming process. It shouldn't take much longer than a quick trim with lever clippers, but using the right tools and techniques will result in healthier, more attractivehands. Enjoy the satisfaction and boost in self-confidence that comes with a job well done.

15

Put the Suds to the Duds

Do you do your own laundry? Or do you drop your dirty clothes into a laundry shoot and they magically reappear in your closet later? Or perhaps someone comes into your room and scoops up all the laundry from your bedroom floor (and under your bed) and then it magically reappears in your closet later?

Regardless of of your current situation, I can almost guarantee that the first scenario - doing your own laundry- is the only one that may be permanent. You will, at some time, need to be able to wash your own clothes. The sooner you learn, the better for you!

As a young man, I was lucky enough to have the second scenario. My mother washed my clothes (as long as I took them to the washing machine). She folded them and put them in my drawers. This was great - until I went to college. I didn't have a clue what I was doing.

Doing laundry is not difficult but there are several rules to follow if you want your clothes to get clean, not be ruined, and last longer. Most guys want to their laundry done as quickly, painlessly and cheaply as possible. If you live at home, the cheaply part is easy!

Follow these rules for the best laundry experience.

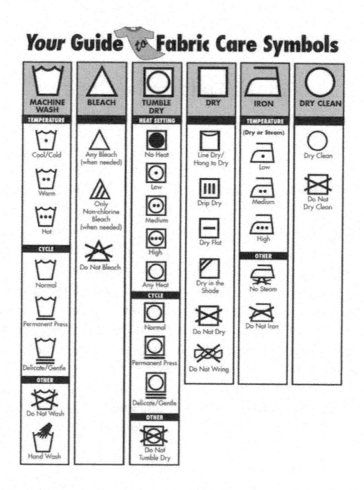

Check the Tag

If your garment has a tag (some shirts don't these days), look for washing instructions. Even shirts without tags will have washing instructions where the tag usually is. You may finds symbols, like in the chart below. Some tags have actual writing on them with special rules like "hand wash," "tumble dry low,"or "hang dry." Follow the instructions and your clothes will thank you for it.

If the tag says "machine wash gentle," it's fine to run a gentle cycle (such as Permanent Press) in the same load with other, tougher clothes.

Most clothes that go beyond the basic cotton or polyester blend (wool, linen, silk, and anything expensive or shiny) have some special instructions.

If it Says "Dry Clean Only," Get it Dry Cleaned

This is important. Dry cleaning is expensive — hence the saying "took me to the cleaners." But it's worth it. If you put a "Dry Clean Only" garment into the the washing machine, it will never be the same.

You probably don't have many items that need to be dry cleaned, so don't worry about the extra money. The bonus is that dry cleaned clothes come back clean, pressed, and looking sharp. It's not a bad idea to take a shirt in to get "freshened up" for that big job interview.

Separate Colors

Your white shirt and socks may seem white after you wash them with dark clothes. But just go stand next to another guy with a white shirt whose shirt IS white. Everyone will see that your shirt is not really white.

You need to get a hamper with three separate compartments. Put your WHITE clothes in compartment #1. Don't put yellow, light gray, cream, off-white or any other non-white garments in there. Stripes are okay as long as the article is mainly white. Your non-white clothes should be divided approximately in half: darker vs lighter. Lighter clothes, including anything that might be considered "bright" go into compartment #2. Darker clothes, including all but the most faded jeans, go into compartment #3. New jeans always go in Compartment #3.

Water Temperature

Washing clothes in hot water helps get rid of grease, dust, and fungus. This is particularly good for socks and sheets. Cold water helps prevent colors from "bleeding," or seeping color out into the water. As a general rule, items in Compartment #1 should be washed hot, Compartment #2 is washed warm, and Compartment #3 is washed cold. If that's too complicated, just remember "white hot, cold & dark."

Bleach

You should only use bleach when washing white clothes from Compartment #1. If you have lots of white clothes with stripes, or colorful clothes with white parts get some detergent with color-safe bleach.

Don't pour the bleach directly into the washing machine. Most washing machines have a liquid bleach dispenser on the topside of the washer. Do not put powder in this pan.

It's better to use too little bleach than too much. If you use too much, your clothes smell like chlorine (that "swimming pool" smell) and wear out fast. You should fill (or almost-fill) the little pan once after you've started the water. The pan will slowly drip bleach into your wash load.

The Dryer: Clean the Lint Screen

The lint screen is a little screen on a plastic frame, usually just inside the opening to the dryer, or possibly in the dryer door. It is designed to prevent lint from clogging up the dryer's exhaust hose. You can save time and money by cleaning he lint screen before using the dryer. Just take it out and scrape the lint off into the garbage can.

Don't Overfill Washer or Dryer

You may be inclined to save a a little time or a few quarters by stuffing things into the washer or dryer, but it usually doesn't work. An overfilled washer can become unbalanced which causes it to not wash or spin properly, leaving your clothes soapy and dripping wet.

Overfilling the dryer doesn't allow enough air to dry the clothes, and will take much longer to dry. You will save time and precious quarters by running two medium-sized loads rather than one stuffed too full. Putting your clothes in the dryer one piece at a time and shaking them out a bit helps everything get dry.

Clothes Fade When You Dry Them, so Hang Dry Expensive Stuff

The dryer is hard on your clothing so some things should hang dry. Think fancy jeans and shirts with the "new" look, any natural fabric (cotton, linen, wool, silk, etc.) with a shiny look to it, and anything you want to keep looking extra fresh. You can put it in the dryer for 5 minutes to get the wrinkles out, then hang dry.

You can use a clothes hanger on a doorknob or shower curtain rack to hang dry your clothes. You should roll up heavy clothes, like sweaters, in a towel, press to squeeze out any extra water, then dry them flat.

16

Know How to Fold 'em

I was never very good at doing laundry. When I was in college, I would do my laundry and then bring it back to my room in my laundry basket. When I wanted to wear one of my freshly cleaned shirts, I pulled it out of my laundry basket and it looked like I had pulled it out from under the bed. At that point, I always wished I had taken the extra five minutes to fold my shirts after I washed them.

Did you ever notice how nice the stack of t-shirts looks in the department store? Each shirt is folded nicely so that the front logo is visible and they lie nice and flat.

It feels great to take a shirt like that and put it on. It doesn't look like you pulled it out from under the bed because there are no wrinkles. It even has those fresh fold creases on the sleeves and in across the mid-section. It's a great way to start any day! You have confidence because you know you look good.

Wouldn't it be nice to open your dresser drawer and see all your favorite t-shirts stacked that way? You can. It just takes a tool made from things you have at home and a few minutes after the laundry is done!

Here is what you need to create a shirt folder: 2 A Parts: 31" long by 10" wide corrugated cardboard; Part B: 31" long by 14" wide corrugated cardboard; Part D: 15" long by 10" wide corrugated cardboard; Duct Tape; A sharp knife (or box cutter); and a ruler/yardstick

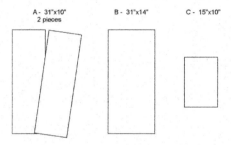

Start by measuring and marking the outline of the four rectangles of sizes above. Then carefully cut them out with your knife. Try to keep the sides as even as possible.

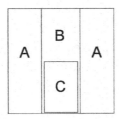

Lay out the panels with the two longer pieces on the outside and two smaller pieces in the center as shown in the illustration. Note the two A Parts are spaced 10" apart. Space them out so that there is a gap of about 1/4 inch between each panel. This gap lets the panels easily fold and move while in use.

Tape A panels to B panel on the front and the back. Then tape the top ¾ of C panel to B panel at the halfway point on the front and back sides. Then your shirt folding board is complete!

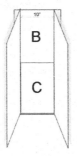

To use your folding board, center the shirt, front down, on the folding board. Fold the right A panel to left, folding the shirt's right third in toward the middle. Then fold right A panel over to the right, folding the shirt's left third in toward the middle so

75

your shirt is folded in the center of board. Flip C panel upward to fold the shirt in half vertically.

Your shirt in now folded and ready to be placed carefully in your drawer. It will be clean and crisp the next time you are ready to wear it and you won't look like you just crawled out from under a rock!

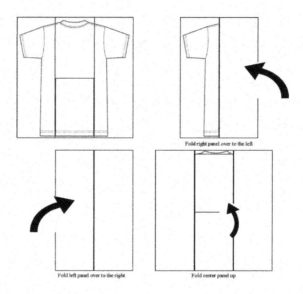

Fold right panel over to the left

Fold left panel over to the right

Fold center panel up

17

Keep a Lid on It!

I don't know a single guy who doesn't have at least 10-12 baseball caps in his closet. The baseball cap is as classic as a pair of blue jeans. Originally worn on baseball fields (hence the name!), it is now a fashion statement that can be worn in different places and occasions.

They are culturally accepted and convenient. A baseball cap is easily packed when not in use. It is a simple solution to keeping the sun off your face, covering up on those bad hair days when you're in a hurry, or showing support of a team, brand or message.

It is a part of our cultural identity. You don't need to be a baseball player or fan to be able to wear this kind of hat. Even basketball and tennis players wear them. It suits many people from many different walks of life.

What to look for in a new cap

Obviously, the primary attraction for most people to buy a new cap is the logo on the front. We'll assume that your favorite team, band, shoe company, etc. makes more than one cap. You probably have some choices.

Less is more when it comes to color and style. You can get a lot more mileage out of a plain black cap or clean white baseball cap than some trendy graffiti-laden lid that will only take you so far and lose its appeal after wearing it for one season.

If you sweat a lot or plan on being in the sun, choose a baseball cap in a breathable fabric such as cotton. Conversely, if you're wearing a cap in the cold, opt for warmer materials such as wool or suede.

How to Break in Your New Cap

The best way to break in a brand new baseball cap is to dampen it with hot water and wear it. While you wear it, curve the bill with your hands to shape it the way you like it. Wear the baseball cap as it air dries so that it conforms to the shape of your head.

Another way to curve the bill on your new baseball cap is to lightly spray it with hot water and gently roll it until it fits inside a large coffee mug. Allow the baseball cap to remain in the mug until it dries and takes the shape you want.

You can get the shape you want by just forming and massaging it as you wear it. Eventually, your new cap will respond to your manipulations and take the shape you want.

Are you a hip-hop star? Keep your bill flat. Everyone else? Bend the sides down.

No Sticker Dicker

Take the sticker on your bill off. We get it. It is new. It was expensive. No matter. You don't leave the tag on your new shirt. Take the sticker off the bill. Anyone worth impressing won't care if it's box fresh.

Buy a Cap That Fits

A baseball cap should feel snug on your head but it should not be so tight that it gives you a headache or leaves indentations on your forehead. If it's adjustable, adjust the cap so it fits. A well-fitting baseball cap should fit on your head so that it will not come off with a wind gust yet won't leave a mark on your forehead. You should be able to easily spin the cap around your head.

A baseball cap should sit comfortably above your ears with the bill resting in the middle of your forehead. The crown of the baseball cap should top your head, leaving a little space between your head and the cap.

The trend today is to wear hats that are several sizes too large. Let's be honest. You look stupid when you wear a cap that is too big. You know when your cap is too big.

If your fitted baseball cap is a little tight, you can dampen the crown of the cap with hot water and place it on the outside of a bowl or pot. As the cap dries, the band of the cap will stretch and get bigger. If it is hopelessly small and you just love it and cannot give it up, you can cut the back seam about a half inch to give yourself some room. You can cut deeper if you need more

79

room, but it's probably time to get a new cap!

If your fitted baseball cap is a little big or loose, you can spray water on the inside and outside of the band (don't spray the section near the brim). Dry the outside of the band with a hair dryer. Then dry the inside of the band. While the band is still slightly damp, place the cap on your head and allow it to air dry as you wear it.

The Direction of Your Cap is the Direction of Your Life

The bill on a baseball cap is a strategic feature of the cap. It was put on the cap to keep the sun out of our eyes. However, you must wear the cap correctly to benefit from this feature.

Unless you are a rap star, point your hat in the direction that you are going. Unless the visor is obstructing your view or preventing you from otherwise safely doing a task, don't wear a baseball cap backwards. It's just not a good look. Same goes for wearing it sideways.

The brim's direction is a projection of you. Be front and center rather than... well, backwards.

My Team, My Brand, My Message

The team, brand or message on the front of your cap may not be your favorite, but others will assume it is! The other day I saw a guy wearing a Boston Red Sox cap. I said, "Go Sox!" Nothing. No response. Blank expression.

I said, "Are you a Red Sox fan? Your hat?" The light bulb flickered on.

He replied, "Oh, no, I just like the hat."

Okay. But everyone, and I mean EVERYONE, will assume that he is a Boston Red Sox fan. Same for Nike, Under Armour, or any other team, message or brand that is on the front of your cap.

Know When to Fold 'Em

Knowing when to where your cap and when to take it off is the difference between a kid and a gentleman. Wearing a cap outdoors, in the sun – good choice. Wearing a cap indoors, with a suit – bad choice!

Although it is very common, you should consider whether or not it is appropriate to wear your cap indoors. There is a difference between wearing a cap at a lively basketball game and a traditional church service.

I believe you should remove your cap any time you visit the home of a friend or family member, in a public places (like restaurants, malls, schools, offices, church, etc.) and during the "National Anthem" (both indoors and outside). You may find other instances when it is appropriate to remove your cap. Generally, it is fine to wear a cap outdoors.

Keep it Clean

You dropped $30 on that cap, take care of it. Hang it up when you're not wearing it. Keep it clean. A grimy hat is never cute unless you're working under a car or truck. Then it's better than grimy hair!

For new cotton, polyester, or mesh hats, pre-treat dirty areas such as sweatbands with a dab of heavy-duty laundry detergent. Work the detergent into the soiled areas with a brush. Allow it to sit for at least 15 minutes before washing.

Throw your cap into a load of similarly colored clothing. Wash using heavy-duty detergent on the delicate cycle, and select cool water. A hat form will protect the shape of your cap in the wash.

Allow the cap to air-dry over a large coffee can or over another head-shaped container. Don't put baseball caps in the dryer because the heat and tumbling action can distort its shape.

Cardboard billed caps (made before the 1980s) leather or wool caps, vintage or commemorative caps should not be washed with the above method. Seek help in getting these cleaned.

The baseball cap is an iconic piece of Americana that has been around for well over 150 years. It will continue to be a wardrobe essential for men and women, young and old.

IV

Skills & Stuff

18

The Drive of Your Life

Cars are part of our American culture. As such, everyone remembers their first car. Some remember their first car for what it was - year, model, make, engine, etc. Others remember their first car for where it took them, the friends who rode shotgun, the responsibilities it brought (or didn't bring) or the sense of freedom that came with it.

For me, it was much more the latter than it was the car. Perhaps if I had driven one of the "muscle cars" of that era, it would be about the car. But my first car was anything but a muscle car. It was closer to an aircraft carrier!

When I got my South Dakota "learner's permit" back in the fall of 1974, I inherited the family station wagon... an imposing 1967 Mercury Colony Park Station Wagon. Before it belonged to my family, it was the property of the Holiday Inn in Mitchell, South Dakota. The wagon bore the remnants of a vinyl sign on its wood-grain side, revealing how the wood grain had endured over time. Even after the vinyl was peeled off, the wood grain underneath remained unaffected, subtly showcasing its connection to the Holiday Inn.

That mattered little to me. Nor was I bothered by the fact that you could land small aircraft on the hood, that the back of the vehicle could house a small family, that it took about 3 gallons of gas to drive a mile (yes that is backwards but gas was about $.35 per gallon, so I didn't think about it), or that it was a "sled.".

Regrettably, I have no photos of the old Mercury, but the image above provides a decent approximation of my car—picture maroon instead of white. (Picture a dimly visible Holiday Inn sign against a faded wood grain backdrop!)

Nonetheless, it was my car—a means to reach my desired destinations. No longer did I have to rely on my bicycle or my parents for rides. I held the optimistic belief that all my fishing gear could easily fit into the wagon's back. What more could a 14-year-old ask for?

Securing your first vehicle brings freedom...AND responsibility. You can make the process much easier if you do your homework and make logical decisions rather than emotional decisions.

Until you have a steady job and stable income, you should not borrow money for a car. Buy a cheap vehicle that will serve your transportation needs.

Establish a Realistic Budget

It's tempting to focus on your car payments but the cost of car ownership includes so much more. You must focus on transportation costs which include the cost of fuel ($65-75/month for 1000 miles), maintenance ($25-100/month), repairs, insurance ($50-65/month), taxes and other miscellaneous costs.

Do you intend to finance your vehicle?

Do you have established credit?

Do you have a down payment?

How much can you afford monthly?

Will the vehicle last that long?

These are all considerations as you look at how you will purchase that vehicle. Even without a car payment, transportation expenses persist. The vehicle you select impacts these associated costs.

Determine Your Transportation Needs

There is a difference between needs and wants and you have to acknowledge the difference between a logical and emotional decision. Someday, you can purchase a vehicle that has all the features and benefits you would like. But your first car will probably be less than that.

Your first vehicle should be a reliable vehicle that will get you where you want to go when you want to go there. Anything beyond that is likely costing you more money than you need to pay (or can afford, perhaps).

Do Your Research

It's never been easier to research the reliability, repair costs, fuel economy, insurance costs and more for vehicles you may be considering. An internet connection is all you need to find sites dedicated to such research.

It's not a bad idea to ask friends or family for their experience. That might even present an opportunity to buy a car you know has been cared for from a friend or family member.

Locate a Trustworthy Dealer or Salesperson

So many people are afraid of dealing with a professional car salesperson. The vast majority of these professionals are trustworthy and can be extremely helpful. They have resources available to them that you may not. They can help find your vehicle. They can help transport it to you if necessary. They can run tests to check the condition. If you can find a salesperson you trust, they can save you time, money, heartache, hassles, and more.

Take a test drive

It is important to determine that the car you are considering is right for you. No deal is a good deal if the vehicle does not work for you. Nothing is more important in your decision process than how you feel behind the wheel.

Seat height, wheel adjustment, steering feel, outward visibility, and control layout all factor into how the vehicle fits you. There's no way to figure it out without spending a reasonable amount of time driving the car. Take at least half an hour, while trying stop-and-go, merging and interstate speeds.

Determine the proper purchase price

Once you've decided what you like — and have already established what you can afford — it's time to arrive at a purchase price. There are online resources that give you an accurate idea of what people have paid for a similar vehicle.

When it's time to replace your first vehicle, you may have further considerations. Do you buy new or used? Is buying or leasing is a better option (in the meantime, take care of your credit). How much for your trade and - do I trade or sell my vehicle?

Until then, though, have fun! Enjoy the process.

19

Spare Me!

A flat tire is inevitable. You can be assured it will come at the most inopportune time! But there are a few things you can do to make it a bit more unlikely that you'll be stranded alongside the road.

Inspect your tires for uneven wear and signs of sidewall damage such as cracks, cuts, chips, and bulges that can contribute to a flat tire if left unchecked. Make sure the tires are inflated to the right pressure by using a tire pressure gauge to check the inflation level on every tire, including the spare. Rotate your tires every 5,000 miles.

Even if you do these things, you're likely to get a flat tire at some point. Knowing how to change a tire is a great skill to have but, sometimes, calling for emergency assistance makes more sense than changing your own tire. Pouring rain, blowing snow, or even blazing heat might make conditions such that you should get help.

For many drivers, suddenly getting a flat while driving, especially on an open highway, is a complete nightmare. It's scary, it's stressful, and it's inconvenient to have your plans derailed to deal with your vehicle's issues.

A sudden flat tire isn't anything to worry about, even though it's inconvenient. Here are a few tips on what you can do and when to call for roadside assistance.

Be Prepared

You should know if your car has a spare tire or a "fix-a-flat" kit. Many newer cars don't come with a spare tire for various reasons, so check to make sure you have one. Check to see that you have a jack and a lug wrench as well.

Periodically check your equipment to make sure you are prepared for an emergency. Be certain your spare is properly inflated and that your jack is in good condition. As for other items you might want to keep in the vehicle: a flashlight/headlamp, tire gauge, and paper towels should suffice. Wheel wedges and a portable tire inflator can be helpful as well.

Waiting to learn how to use your tools on a dark, rainy night can be frustrating and dangerous. Consider doing a practice run when your tire is not flat so you can get a feel for how to perform the task.

Don't Continue To Drive

The worst thing you can do when you notice a flat tire is to continue to drive on it. You can cause further tire damage beyond repair. Driving on a flat tire can cause damage to the rims and other damage like brake lines, rotors, and suspension.

Try to find a level, hard surface with separation between the road and the car. Do not park on dirt or grass if possible - your jack may sink into the dirt and become unstable. Try to avoid hills to prevent your car from rolling. Turn on the flashers on while navigating to your chosen spot. Once there, set your parking brake. Place wheel wedges against both wheels opposite the one that is flat.

Pry off the Wheel Cover

You can use a screwdriver to pry the wheel cover off. Just insert the point of the tool where the edge of the cover meets the wheel, and apply a little leverage. The cap should pop off. You may have to do this in a couple of places, as if you were prying the lid off a can of paint.

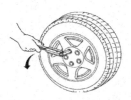

Loosen the Lugs

You may need to pry off a lug nut cover, but most of the time you can get right to business. Loosen the lugs slightly before you jack up your vehicle by turning the nut counterclockwise. Don't remove the lug nuts completely; just get them loose enough to remove by hand after you jack up the vehicle

If you have alloy wheels that are held on by lug nuts with delicate finishes, the delicate aluminum or chrome-plated lug nuts need careful handling. They should never be loosened or replaced with power tools that can scratch the delicate finish. You may need a lug key adapter for one or all of the lugs depending on your vehicle.

Lift Up Your Car

Consult with your owner's manual for the best place to secure you jack, and follow those directions carefully! If you have a scissor jack, insert the rod or wrench over the knob, and then crank. If you have a hydraulic jack, place the handle into the appropriate location and pump up and down. Crank your car up just enough for the tire to lift off the ground to remove the flat tire.

Remove the Lug Nuts and Wheel

Spin the already loosened lug nuts the rest of the way off and put them somewhere safe. Then, remove the wheel from the car. Ideally, it'll just fall right off, but a few well-placed kicks to the sidewall from the right angle can break it free if it's being stubborn.

Mount the Spare

Get out your spare. For most cars and SUVs, it'll be under the loading floor. Trucks might keep it suspended under the bed, but there will likely be a center nut holding it in place that you'll have to unscrew to free it regardless of its location.

Ensure that the vehicle is lifted enough to get the tire onto the wheel. Place the spare tire in front of the wheel well, align it with the wheel bolts. Then lift it into place and add your lug nuts. Turn the lug nuts clockwise by hand as tightly as possible. Then take your wrench and turn the bolt tight enough to secure the tire before lowering it to the ground. Do not tighten them completely yet.

Lower Your Vehicle – Part 1

Slowly lower your vehicle to the ground so that the spare tire is just resting on the ground; the full weight of the car should not yet be on it.

Tighten the Lugs

Arguably the most important job is making sure you tighten all the lugs down nice and snug. Tighten them in a crisscross pattern, going across - not in a circle - when you change the lug you're wrenching on. This helps ensure the lugs are tightened down evenly.

Repeat this process a couple times to make sure you have them as tight they can be. You most likely won't have a torque wrench with you, so just make sure they feel snug and you should be good to go.

Lower Your Vehicle – Part 2

Now you can lower your vehicle so that its full weight is on the ground.

Replace the Wheel Cover

If your car has wheel covers with a delicate finish, the owner's manual should provide instructions for replacing it. If your car has hubcaps, place the hubcap against the wheel and whack it into place with the heel of your hand. Cushion your hand with a soft rag first so that you won't hurt it. Don't hit the hubcap with a wrench or hammer — you'll dent it.

Clean Up and Drive Home

Gather up all the tools you've been using plus your flat tire and secure them in the trunk. Wipe your hands off a bit to avoid smearing tar and dirt all over your interior.

Driving on a tiny space saver spare is different than your regular tire. Most of the time the tires are only rated for a max speed of 50-55 mph. The car will handle and brake much differently, too, so be cautious and feel out the new driving dynamics of the tiny tire. Space savers are only designed to travel a low number of miles, so you're going to want a new tire ASAP.

20

Prevention is the Best Medicine

When it comes to car ownership, there are four essential aspects to consider: car payment (if applicable), fuel, insurance, and maintenance. Regular vehicle maintenance includes an important task: changing the engine oil. Doing it yourself can save you money on oil change costs and is a vital part of vehicle upkeep that you can easily perform at home.

How Often?

How often should you change your oil? If you're using conventional oil, it is recommended to change it every 3,000 to 5,000 miles. Synthetic oil allows for longer intervals between changes. For more specific guidelines based on your vehicle, consult your owner's manual.

To ensure you're following the right schedule, it's crucial to differentiate between normal and severe driving conditions. Sometimes, seemingly mild driving situations can fall under severe conditions. For example, short trips with a 20-year-old car like Grandma's, despite having only 18,000 miles, can be considered severe due to the frequent stops. Be mindful of your driving conditions to determine the appropriate interval for oil changes. Following these guidelines will save you money in the long run and keep your car reliable.

Safety First

Safety should always be your top priority. While most vehicles follow similar steps for changing oil and oil filters, there may be variations depending on your vehicle. Consider referencing a repair guide or seeking information from where you purchase your oil, oil filter, tools, and safety equipment like nitril gloves and safety goggles.

Oil comes in different weights and types, and each vehicle requires a specific amount. Consult your vehicle's owner's manual to ensure you purchase the right oil and filter. It's recommended to drain warm oil so, if it's cold outside, run the car for a bit. If it's been running, allow it to cool before proceeding.

To access the bottom of the engine easily, it's preferable to raise the front of the vehicle using jack stands or drive the vehicle up onto weight-bearing ramps. Both of these items can be found at your local auto parts store. If you're not lifting the vehicle, park it on a flat surface, engage the parking brake, and use wheel chocks behind the rear wheels. Remember to wear gloves and safety goggles throughout the process.

Draining the oil

To drain the oil, open the hood and remove the oil filler cap. Locate the drain plug underneath your vehicle, usually positioned at the lowest part of the engine, and place a pan underneath it. Use a wrench to remove the drain plug and allow the oil to drain into the pan. Inspect the plug and plug gasket for

97

any damage or wear and replace them if necessary. You can find replacements at your local auto parts store. Let the oil drain until it slows to a slow drip, then clean the oil drain plug and reinstall it, being careful not to over-tighten and risk damaging the threads or causing leaks.

Remove and Replace the Filter

Next, remove and replace the oil filter. Position the pan under the filter and remove it. Oil will start to come out and fall into the pan. Depending on the type of filter, there are tools available at your local auto parts store for removal. Always use a new oil filter designed to last the life of the oil you're using. Ensure that the old filter's gasket was removed with the filter to create a proper seal with the new filter. Wipe the filter mount, lubricate the seal on a spin-on filter, or the O-ring on a cartridge filter. Install the new filter, making sure not to over-tighten.

Refill Oil

Finally, it's time to refill the oil. Consult your owner's manual for the volume of oil your vehicle requires. Use a funnel and add the correct amount of new oil, being careful not to overfill. Remove the dipstick, wipe it clean, re-insert and then remove it again to check the oil level. Ensure that you have the proper amount of oil in your engine. When you've got the proper amount, put the dipstick back in, replace the engine oil cap, and check for any leaks. Ensure that the cap, drain plug, and oil filter are securely tightened.

Start the engine, let it run for a few minutes, then turn it off and let it sit. Check the oil level once again by removing, wiping, re-inserting, and inspecting the dipstick. You may need to top off the oil if necessary. Double-check for any possible leaks.

Finishing the Job

Finish the job by cleaning up any spilled oil and resetting the vehicle's oil maintenance reminder, if applicable. Instructions for resetting the dashboard indicator can be found in your owner's manual. Place a reminder sticker on the windshield to keep track of the next oil change. These stickers are available at your local auto parts store. Additionally, if you maintain a vehicle maintenance journal, record the date and mileage of the oil change. A journal can help document your vehicle's maintenance history, which can enhance its value when it comes time to sell or trade it.

Always dispose of automotive fluids properly. Transfer the used motor oil into a container that can be securely closed and take it to a recycling facility for safe disposal.

21

Mow-tivation

What if you could start your own business today with low startup costs, lots of flexibility, high demand for your service, recurring revenue from repeat customers, learn new skills, the opportunity to develop new relationships and offer the chance to grow as big as you'd like? Mowing lawns can be a fulfilling and profitable venture for a young man willing to put in the effort and manage a business responsibly.

One of the ways to differentiate yourself from other young entrepreneurs is to edge the lawn, trim the lawn, and blow of driveways and sidewalks clean when you're done. Your customers should barely know you were there!

Before you start, ensure your equipment is properly cared for . Check the gas and oil. Keep your mower blade sharp. It is important that you sharpen the mower blades at the first sign of wear. Dull blades tear up grass, causing ragged, brown edges. Check your weed eater, edger and leaf blower condition as well.

Know how to start your equipment. Each mower, edger, weed eater and blower is a little different. Most mowers require you to choke it. Choke it once and when you're done, push back in and turn up the speed. Also don't forget to take the brake off when ready to move. Nothing is more frustrating than not being able to start equipment when you need it.

Another thing to check before you begin is to make sure the lawnmower is set at the correct height. You will typically want a three inch blade height. You should not mow more than one third of the height of the grass, however. A healthy lawn can survive an occasional close cut but routine close mowing is very hard on the grass and produces a brown lawn.

You should mow only when it is dry enough. It is usually difficult to mow in the morning because lawns are wet from dew. The best time of day to mow a lawn is in the early evening. Mowing when temperatures are highest stresses both the lawn and, of course, you. If you wait until the early evening, the lawn is usually dry (unless it has rained during the day), the sun is less intense, and the lawn will have plenty of time to recover before the next afternoon's heat arrives.

Cutting wet grass can result in an uneven trim. Wet clippings can also clog your mower and cause it to dump clumps of grass on your lawn. If those clumps aren't raked up, they can smother the growing grass and result in brown spots.

Before mowing, it is important to check for any debris that may be on the lawn, because foreign objects can damage the lawn mower. It can also create a missile when discharged from the mower.

Start by make two passes around the edge of the lawn. Overlap the passes'; there will be uncut areas of lawn if there isn't enough overlap. Remember that the grass shoots to the right side of the mower so start on the left outline and try not to spray the house, car, shed, etc. with the grass. You want to discharge the clippings (unless you bag them) towards the area you've already cut.

It is important to alternate the mowing direction each time the lawn gets mowed. Mowing in the same pattern every time can cause excessive wear, or damage the lawn. Mow in a different direction each time you mow. If you don't, your grass will start to lean in the direction you mow and you may even end up with ruts in the lawn. Grass will stand up nice and tall since it will be mowed from all different directions as well.

If you can convince your lawn owner, leave the grass clippings on the lawn. Grass clippings break down quickly and return beneficial nutrients to the soil. You should have a mulching blade on your mower if you are going to do this. Be sure to mow often enough that you're not removing too much at once and the clippings are small. Shaving off too much of the grass blade shocks the grass and leaves piles of long clippings that don't break down quickly and can smother growing grass. If you do end up bagging your clippings, toss them in the garden as mulch, or compost them.

Cut the grass around flower beds, trees, and any areas the mower was unable to mow at approximately the same height as the mower. Be careful not to damage the bark at the base of the trees, and do not cut the grass too low or damage will occur. Once you have finished mowing, look to see if it may be need to cut twice, if there are clumps of grass, or it just doesn't look good.

- *Edger* – An edger is a tool that cuts the grass that grows over the concrete on the sides of the driveways and walk ways. It also needs to be choked when started along with the rest of the tools.
- String trimmer – Trim with string trimmer over the edged

grass because, after you edge it, the grass tends to stand noticeably taller. Also string trim areas which the mower could not reach: sides of houses, around trees, sheds, flower beds, etc.

- Leaf blower - Finally, grab a leaf blower and blow off any unwanted grass and remaining dirt from the street, sidewalk, drive way, walk ways, or gardents. It's okay to leave the clippings in the grass. You aren't going to do any harm by leaving the clippings out there.

Safety Items

- *Wear the proper footwear* - Sandals are not proper footwear for mowing the lawn. They're less stable, and a trip, slip or stumble could cause you to come in contact with moving or hot parts.
- *Watch out for kids* – You must pay attention when pushing a mower around the yard. Kids can get in the way. Be careful!

- *Avoid yard missiles* - Pick up stones, branches, toys, sprinklers and other items before you start mowing. If you miss something and notice it while you're mowing, pick it up right away.
- *Don't mow over gravel* - Never cross over a gravel driveway with the blades engaged. Mow grass near gravel only when there are no cars or pedestrians passing by.
- *Don't pull backward* - Whenever possible, try not to pull a lawn mower toward you. If you slip, you could end up pulling the mower right on top of you.
- *Wear hearing protection* - Exposure to sounds over 85 decibels for extended time periods can cause hearing damage. Lawn mowers can produce more than 100 decibels—wear hearing protection.
- *Keep clear of moving blades* - If the blades are spinning, don't unclog the chute, adjust the wheel height, inspect the blades or do anything that would bring your appendages in harm's way.

Maintenance

Keep your mower in great condition. Even when you are not using your lawn mower it is important to keep your mower well-maintained throughout the year. Just like your car, you need to be sure that all the parts of your mower are working correctly before you start the cutting process.

A mower tune-up and blade sharpening once a year is a great idea. Your mower will start easier, make cleaner cuts, and slice your clippings without bogging down the mower blades.

Remember to wash your mower after each use, to help prevent any blockages within the mower itself.

22

Do You Believe in Magic?

Why do I want to practice magic?

Performing magic helps you build confidence in yourself. A magician needs an audience. Each time you perform your tricks, you become more confident with your magic and yourself.

Not everyone is capable of presenting in front of a group of people. It is a wonderful life skill that can help you in so many ways. Performing magic will also help you to develop your presentation and communication skills.

You can instantly become the life of any party or social gathering if you can entertain a crowd with a few magic tricks. Magic is the perfect icebreaker when you meet someone for the first time which will ensure that you always leave a positive first impression.

Magic, like music, is a universal language and can be enjoyed by anyone regardless of where you come from. You can over-come language barriers by showing them a magic trick. It will help you to build an instant connection without even saying a word!

Magic allows you to transport your audience to a place where nothing is impossible. Through magic, you can create a moment of pure wonder, during which all of life's stresses and strains seem to float away. Magic is a way to make people smile. That is an opportunity you never want to miss!

Why people love magic

Magic is one of the oldest and most successful performing arts. It started as a form of entertainment at fairs in the 19th century. These days, magic is seen everywhere from TV shows and theaters to corporate parties and children's birthdays – it's impossible not to love it. It would be very hard to find someone who doesn't enjoy a good magic act. But why are people so drawn to magic? If they weren't, famous magicians like David Copperfield would not have sold tickets worth billions of dollars. Psychologists are a category of scientists who have researched magic and the fascination it provokes to audiences. Here are some of the conclusions researchers have drawn:

People are attracted to things that cannot be explained. Babies love to play Peek-a-Boo. The idea of something appearing and disappearing in front of them intrigues babies and makes them curious. That's the same feeling adults get when they see magic performed.

We like to think it may be possible for some unbelievable things to happen, such as people levitating or teleporting themselves to Hawaii. A part of us wants to believe that magic is real: even highly educated people end up believing some magicians have special skills for reading the minds of their audience.

The main reason why magicians don't reveal their tricks is that people are no longer amazed when they find out how a trick is performed. Never reveal your secrets!

Magic is not just about special actions and tricks that seem impossible. A sense of magic can also be found in a book that captivates us, in falling in love, or in enjoying a delicious desert. The special effects we see in the movies are also a form of magic or trickery.

When we were young, many of the things we observed around us were unexplained, just like magic. As adults, we know a lot more about the way the world is functioning, but sometimes we need that feeling of not being able to explain facts. Magic can be a way to keep hope, as the sense of wonder it produces l makes us feel happy. Magic is a way to escape from the painful reality of life by ceasing to believe in reality and entering the illusion of magic.

Because we need to make sense of the world around us, when some facts are impossible to explain, we "blame" it on magic and the dilemma is solved! Moreover, we like to think humans have destinies, that symbols have power, that objects can have a life of their own, and there is something special about each one of us.

Magical thinking will probably never disappear, because it is a safety mechanism. When something happens, we tend to assume the event was caused by *something* - whether we're speaking about a rabbit coming out of a hat or falling in love at first sight with a complete stranger we met by chance.

As a magician, your job is to transport your audience to a place where nothing is impossible. Magic can help create a moment of pure wonder and joy. It can make all of life's stresses and strains float away for a little while. Ultimately, we get to make people smile, and it really does not get much better than that.

V

Leadership & Stuff

23

Dream Big (and Write it Down!)

I was probably close to thirty years old before I learned the power of writing down my goals and rereading them regularly. Prior to that, I had learned that it was important to have goals but did not understand the power of committing them to paper.

I recently came across some of the goals I'd written down over thirty years ago. I had three goals in each of three categories – personal, professional and family. It is so interesting to look back at those goals and see that I accomplished almost all of them. I may not have achieved them in the time I specified then, but I can see that writing them down made them happen!

I wrote a chapter about goals and setting goals in *Man Stuff: Things a Young Man Needs to Know* ("*With a Goal In Mind*"), but I believe the topic is so important, I'm including another chapter here. Here we'll look at how dreams and goals are both important, but different.

What's the difference between dreams and goals?

Dreams and goals are both ideas related to achieving something you desire. They differ in their characteristics and how you pursue them. A dream is something you contemplate the possibility of achieving or attaining. You think about it but you don't take any concrete action toward it.

Dreams are important because they can inspire you to aim higher, reach for your potential, and aspire to achieve things you may have thought were impossible. They can motivate you to take action and work towards your goals. They allow you to use your imagination and creativity to envision new possibilities and explore different ideas. Dreams can help you solve problems and work through challenges in your life.

Goals are different from dreams in that they provide focus and direction to prioritize your time and energy towards achieving what is important to you. Without goals, it is easy to get distracted by the many responsibilities in your daily life.

Goals provide motivation, giving you a reason to take action and work towards achieving something that you want or need. The sense of progress and accomplishment that comes with achieving a goal can be highly rewarding.

Goals provide clarity and help you to define what you want to achieve, how you will achieve it, and when you will achieve it. This clarity can help you make better decisions and take more purposeful actions in your life.

Goals can help you to grow and develop as an individual, challenging you to step outside of your comfort zone and learn new skills or behaviors in the process of achieving your goals.

Goals provide a measure of accountability, helping you track your progress and hold yourself accountable for taking the necessary actions to achieve your desired outcomes.

Overall, goals are essential for personal and professional growth, providing a road map for achieving what is important to us and helping us to live more purposeful and fulfilling lives.

**A GOAL IS
A DREAM
WITH A
DEADLINE.**

NAPOLEON HILL

How do you set goals?

Because a goal is a pledge to yourself, it is written down and accompanied by a plan. Start by defining what you want to achieve. Be specific, and write down your goal in clear and concise language. Make sure that your goal is realistic and achievable within a reasonable time frame.

Goals can be categorized as long-term and short-term. Long-term goals take a year or longer to achieve. Short-term goals can be accomplished in three months to a year. Short-term goals can be used as steps to achieving long-term goals.

Short term goals should be specific, measurable, achievable, relevant and have a deadline.

- **Specific** – What is it that you want to accomplish?
- **Measurable** – How will you know that you have been successful?
- **Achievable** – Is achieving this goal realistic? What are the steps involved in accomplishing this goal? Are there any constraints and requirements that you need to consider?
- **Relevant** – Does this short-term goal serve your long-term goals? Is achieving this goal worth the time and effort?

113

- **Deadline** – How long will it take to accomplish this goal? When would you like to have completed this goal? Are there any external time constraints?

You should use these parameters when setting short term goals.

They can stand alone or they can be steps that move you closer to your long term goals.

Dreams are things we imagine or aspire to achieve, but they may not have a clear plan or timeline to achieve them. Dreams can be seen as more abstract, emotional and often don't have a specific or measurable outcome. Dreams can inspire and motivate us, but they do not necessarily require action or effort to make them a reality.

On the other hand, goals are specific, measurable, and time-bound objectives that require action and planning to achieve them. Goals are often seen as more concrete and achievable, and they require a clear plan with actionable steps to reach them. Goals can be used to break down bigger dreams into smaller, more manageable tasks that can be accomplished in a shorter time frame.

Break it down: Once you have defined your goal, break it down into smaller, more manageable steps. This will make your goal seem less overwhelming and help you create a clear plan of action.

Set a deadline: Set a deadline for when you want to achieve your goal. This will help you stay focused and motivated, and it will give you a clear sense of urgency to work towards your goal.

Make a plan: Create a step-by-step plan for how you will achieve your goal. This plan should include the smaller steps you identified in step 2, as well as any resources or support you will need to achieve your goal.

Track your progress: Keep track of your progress towards your goal. This will help you stay motivated and identify any obstacles or challenges you may need to overcome.

Adjust your plan as needed: As you work toward your goal, you may need to adjust your plan based on new information or changes in circumstances. Be flexible and willing to make changes as needed to ensure you stay on track towards achieving your goal.

Remember, setting goals is a powerful tool for achieving success in any area of your life. By following these steps and staying focused and committed, you can achieve your goals and create the life you want.

In 2019, I decided that I wanted to learn how to play the guitar. I knew that would require consistent practice. I set a short-term goal of fifteen minutes of practice per evening knowing that would help me achieve the long-term goal of playing the guitar. I bought a guitar stand so I could display the guitar in such a way that would constantly remind me of my goal.

As I practiced, my short-term goals became more specific and focused as my long-term goal evolved into learning blues guitar. After about a year, my long-term goals became more specific so I had to adjust my short-term goals to match. I wanted to learn the 12-bar blues rhythm and learn some blues lead licks. My short-term practice habits had to change to support those long-term goals.

I am no blues guitar master, but after almost four years, I can entertain myself and my grandchildren with my guitar.

24

What I Think I Think

Journaling is the act of writing down thoughts, experiences, reflections, and emotions in a personal journal or diary. It is a form of self-expression and self-reflection that can be done in various formats, including handwritten or typed entries, digital documents, drawing, collages, sketches, pictures, newspaper clippings, photographs, paintings, scribbling or even audio recordings.

You can gain a more positive view on your life by developing an awareness of events, memories and feelings in your life through keeping a journal. You can learn how to handle life challenges, use your imagination and creative talents, and improve your communication skills. Journaling activities can also help you gain insights into relationships with your peers, parents and other adults, and help you better understand your body and health issues.

Journaling can be used for many purposes

- **Self-reflection**: Many people use journaling as a means to explore their thoughts and feelings, gain insight into their emotions, and better understand themselves. By writing down their innermost thoughts and reflections, individuals can gain clarity, process their emotions, and gain a deeper understanding of their own experiences.

- **Creativity**: Journaling can be a tool for enhancing creativity. It provides a space for brainstorming ideas, capturing inspiration, and exploring new perspectives. Many writers, artists, and other creative individuals use journaling as a way to express themselves and generate new ideas.
- **Emotional well-being**: Journaling can serve as an emotional outlet, allowing individuals to release their thoughts and feelings onto the page. It can help manage stress, reduce anxiety, and promote emotional well-being by providing a safe space to express and process emotions.
- **Goal setting and planning**: Journaling can be used as a tool for setting and tracking personal goals. By writing

down specific goals, creating action plans, and reflecting on progress, individuals can use journaling as a means of motivation and accountability.

· **Memory keeping**: Journaling can be a way to document and preserve memories. Many people use journals to record significant life events, travel experiences, and everyday moments to create a personal record that can be cherished and revisited in the future.

How to Journal

Find a comfortable, relaxing and quiet setting, free from interruptions and distractions. You may like to observe a few minutes of silence before you begin to focus your attention. You may prefer low background music.

If you are tense in any way, take a deep breath and try to relax. Plan to spend at least 10 minutes journaling. If you don't have at least 10 minutes, you may benefit from waiting until you have more time. Don't put pressure on yourself. It's okay if you miss a day or two.

You can explore something that's bothering you, write about the present moment, or play with a prompt. You may choose to write about people, events, things or feelings that are prominent in your life right now. You may write in a "stream of consciousness," which is simply thoughts going through your mind, without regard to form.

You may choose to create a list of things, feelings, people or events. You may use pictures, drawings, cartoons or photos to express thoughts or feelings. You might review previous journal entries and reflect on past thoughts. There are no rules.

Journaling can take many forms, depending on individual preferences and needs. Some people may write in their journal daily, while others may do so sporadically or when they feel the need to express themselves. There are no strict rules for journaling - it should be a flexible practice that can adapt to suit your needs and goals.

Privacy is an important aspect of journaling. Your journal should be kept in a safe, private place. Date your entries so the journal becomes a personal history of growth and experience. Don't worry about spelling, grammar, penmanship or punctuation. You can save that for English class!

Like any skill, the more often you journal, the better you become at it. Journaling on a regular basis is the best way to gain the skill.

Ideas for Journal Content

- How would you describe yourself?
- How would your friends describe you?
- How would you like to be described?
- What are you especially proud of about yourself?
- What are you the least proud of about yourself?
- Think of a person in your life. What is this person like?
- How do you find joy being with this person?
- How are you similar to this person or not?
- Add pictures or drawings, give titles or comment on them.

Journaling has a range of benefits. Just writing a few minutes a day may help reduce stress, boost your well-being, and better understand your needs.

25

In Giving We Receive

I serve as an advisor to a service club for young men who are middle school students. One of the club's members was using a wheelchair, and his friends wanted to support his family in acquiring a new wheelchair. However, his family proposed a broader initiative: they suggested that the group lead an effort to construct a wheelchair ramp at the local marina. This ramp would enhance accessibility to the Missouri River for all individuals using wheelchairs.

To fund this endeavor, the young men in the group undertook various chores around the community, accepting "free will" contributions for their efforts. They engaged in tasks like raking leaves, cleaning house gutters, washing windows, moving furniture, and performing other necessary duties.

With the funds they raised, totaling around $5,000, the group contributed towards the acquisition and installation of a ramp. This ramp facilitates easier access for individuals in wheelchairs or with mobility challenges to reach their boats and the river. The ramp features a mesh sling for loading and unloading. The person using a wheelchair is positioned onto the sling, which then lifts them up and pivots toward the boat. By cranking the sling, the person is gently lowered into the boat. The same ramp and sling are used to disembark from the boat as well.

This area in South Dakota is a popular spot for fishing and recreation. This ramp and device could be the sole one of its kind in the state. Consequently, it's anticipated that more people will visit the community to access the water, which will then benefit local businesses.

As these young men witness people utilizing the ramp, they'll forever remember the dedicated work they invested in this project. They'll recognize the number of individuals who will benefit from this effort and gain access to the water.

Stewardship
Leaving things better than you found them

Have you ever taken a moment to pick up a piece of litter from the ground? Or spent some of your time to assist those in need? Have you stood up against bullying and advocated for an inclusive atmosphere at school? Perhaps you've participated in events within your neighborhood or school that promote positive change.

Each of these actions exemplifies stewardship. A steward

is someone who takes responsibility for something entrusted to them. As stewards, we cultivate greater consideration for our environment, our decisions, and our role in the world. Stewardship fuels our passion for taking better care of what the world has bestowed upon us, ensuring that future generations can also appreciate it.

Stewardship extends to treating others with kindness and respect, exhibiting leadership through our actions, and making constructive contributions to our community. In essence, it entails being vigilant caretakers of both our planet and the people who inhabit it.

Sharing your talents is one way to practice stewardship. Whether it's singing, creating artwork, fixing things, or excelling in athletics, these talents can be shared with others. Another approach is to utilize resources responsibly and efficiently to achieve the most favorable outcomes for people, the environment, and the economy. This involves being mindful of how our resource consumption impacts the environment and society at large.

What are some additional ways to practice stewardship?

- Recycling paper, plastic, and glass to minimize waste.
- Turning off lights and electronics when not in use to conserve energy.
- Using reusable water bottles and lunch containers to reduce single-use plastics.
- Participating in community clean-up events to maintain local parks and streets.
- Planting trees or nurturing community gardens to enhance green spaces.
- Be mindful of water usage by taking shorter showers,

turning off the water when you brush your teeth and fixing leaks.

- Learning about local wildlife and ecosystems and refrain from disturbing them.
- Supporting initiatives aimed at protecting endangered species and their habitats.
- Treating classmates, teachers, and family members with kindness and respect.
- Completing household chores responsibly, demonstrating care for personal spaces and belongings.
- Keeping school supplies organized and in good condition to reduce waste.
- Exhibiting punctuality and reliability, building trust among peers.
- Encouraging friends to adopt eco-friendly habits and participate in community service.
- Serving as a positive role model by showcasing responsible behavior and wise decision making.
- Backing local businesses and community projects to fortify the local economy.
- Expanding your knowledge of environmental issues, sustainability, and social justice.
- Sharing newfound knowledge with friends and family to inspire positive actions.
- Engaging in discussions about global challenges and brainstorming solutions.
- Demonstrating respect and responsibility online, refraining from cyberbullying and negativity.
- Using technology judiciously, managing screen time, and employing energy-saving settings.
- Gaining insight into money management, making prudent

spending choices.
· Grasping the significance of saving and budgeting for future
objectives.

Becoming a better steward is an ongoing journey of enhance-
ment. Regardless of the scale, each effort contributes to a more
conscientious and compassionate world.

26

Teamwork Makes the Dream Work

Despite my love of sports, I was a very average high school athlete. I did not play much varsity basketball until my senior year. I broke my leg playing baseball between my sophomore and junior years. It took me out of football and it shortened my junior basketball season significantly.

Basketball was my favorite sport and I worked hard to get ready for my senior basketball season. I knew we could have a pretty good team.

My teammates voted me a captain despite the fact that I played very little as a junior. Though I started every game my senior year, I was the fifth or sixth best player on that team. But I worked hard in practice every day and I think I earned my teammates' respect.

Our team went 18-3 and, despite the fact that we came up 5 points short of a trip to the state tournament, it was a successful year. We surpassed all expectations and compiled the best record of any team at our school in ten years.

As I reflect on it, I think my basketball teammates chose me as a captain because I was a good teammate - not because I was a great basketball player.

Being a great teammate is far more important than being a great player. Not everyone can be a great player, but EVERYONE can be a great teammate. Being a great teammate is an attitude, not a skill. Being a great teammate is completely unrelated to your ability on the field, or in the office. You have complete control over your attitude.

Being a great teammate is a choice between promoting your-self and your needs, or promoting the needs of the team. Making that choice can sometimes be challenging. We are programmed to do what's best for ourselves.

The people you've worked with or played with may remember if you were a talented contributor. Perhaps.

But they will absolutely remember what kind of teammate you were. You may be the best in the world at what you do, but if you were a bad teammate, people will remember that. Being a great teammate may not always seem important in the competitive moment and, in fact, many mediocre teammates hide behind that "I just want to win" mentality.

But down the road, peoples' recollection of you will be less about what your record was on the field. Rather, their memories of you will be overwhelmingly based on how you treated them and the rest of the team.

People often misunderstand what makes a great team player. Have you ever watched the star player in an interview after the game? This often gives us a glimpse of what kind of teammate they are. If I hear them talk about "I" and "me," I tend to believe they are not as good a teammate as if they talk more about "us" and "we."

We often think of a teammate as one who plays with us on the field or court. But you have teammates on school and work projects, music groups, in the workforce and on community projects. While these "teams" may be different than a sports team, the qualities of a good teammate are the same.

Strong teams, sports or otherwise, tend to be more productive, efficient, and innovative.

Let's also remember that teamwork is proven to improve the morale and overall well-being of employees. This happens because everyone feels valued, trusts one another, and steps up when others need them.

Some people think teamwork or collaboration means saying yes to everything, not having boundaries, and never pushing back on bad ideas. In reality, the opposite is true.

You have the ability to be an intelligent and capable member of a team. That means you shouldn't be afraid of speaking up when needed. In fact, it's probably expected of you. You need to recognize that you're a valuable contributor and can participate in decision-making.

There are several characteristics all good teammates have, whether they play on a sports team, serve on a team at work or are working with others on some other project.

What makes a good teammate?

Commit to the Team
You should be fully invested in your team. A great team player shows others that they believe in the group, the process and the goals. It is important to trust teammates.

Working with a team means there will undoubtedly be varying opinions and ideas. Even if you think your idea is best, you should listen to all ideas before pushing yours. Search for compromises, and remain respectful if your work is criticized.

Most people want to perform well and be recognized for their successes. When you're on a team, it's important to work together towards common goals. You will notice that the "Player of the Year" or "MVP" in most professional sports leagues comes from a championship team. Very seldom is it a member of a losing team. Great team players are interested in not just their own success, but the success of the whole team.

Stay positive

People don't likeworking with negative people. Negativity drains team morale, so it's important to remember that, even when times get tough, you need to work with your team to solve problems that are difficult.

Maintaining a positive attitude will make you a more popular team member, and a more effective one. This is especially true when difficulties occur and challenges arise.

Maintaining a positive attitude even during stressful times helps the rest of your team work through that difficult time without getting upset. Your positive attitude will create a better atmosphere. (See the chapter on *Don't Worry, Be Happy*.)

Communicate with Teammates

Great team players put the team first by communicating openly. Offering constructive criticism and honest feedback helps a team to reach peak performance.

Teammates need to update each other on progress and what you need to be successful in your job or role. You should be in constant communication with your team to ensure that every-one is working toward the same goal and no one is repeating work.

Respectfully and tactfully delivering criticism can be a whole

128

new skill in itself. Try to do it in a way that doesn't place blame and doesn't disrespect or demean your team members - be as kind as possible while still being honest.

Actively listen. Hear and thoughtfully respond to what your team member says. Ask questions about things you don't understand.

Respect

A great teammate respects other teammates, your coaches, your family, your teachers, your facilities, your school, and your fans. Look people in the eye. Nod and acknowledge your coach when they are addressing you. Clean up after yourself. Be polite. Encourage your teammates. Help create a culture of mutual respect.

Understand your role on the team

As a team member, you must understand your role on the team and work to achieve your duties to the best of your ability. Though you may offer help or solutions to other team members, you also respect the boundaries of your position.

Remember that no job is too small. Teams succeed when teammates can count on each other to fulfill their role, regardless of how important it seems.

Great team players don't let their ego get in the way. Arrogance will lose the respect of your team members and will have a negative effect on team performance. You should approach every contribution you make to your team with a positive attitude. Every little effort helps and even the smallest tasks can make a big impact.

When you work in a team, you have to be ready to face change. Roles may change, goals may shift and great team players are ready for it. Being flexible and adapting where necessary are crucial when working on your own or as part of a team. The fact of the matter is that you can never control everything, but you can be ready to tackle anything.

You are Flexible

You should readily accept any tasks your coach or manager gives you. Flexibility in your role allows you to learn more and help your team. Look at every opportunity as a chance to learn.

Own Mistakes and Find Solutions.

Understand how your actions impact the entire group. In doing so, you will learn from your errors and command more respect from your team. Never places blame or find excuses.

Be a cheerleader

Celebrate your teammates' successes. If a member of your team succeeds, so do you. It means you are one step closer to completing a goal. Also, stay updated on their personal lives and take the time to express interest and care.

Offer help. If you see a coworker who seems overwhelmed or is struggling to keep up with tasks, ask if you can help. Team players support each other during difficult times. Remember to ask for help when you need it as well.

A great teammate is optimistic. A positive mental attitude keeps morale high. Teams value people who exude optimism. Don't be a player constantly complaining to others about what's wrong.

Look for the positives in your teammates and coaches. Then tell them! Let them know the things they do well. Everyone likes to hear good things about themselves. Find the good. Find the reason for hope when all seems hopeless.

Work Hard and Do your Best

Great team players show initiative and take steps to help lead their team to the next level. A team of robots that simply do what is asked of them is not going to grow and develop. You should use team meetings and engagement to help generate new ideas, stimulate outside thinking and take action. Taking a proactive approach to improving your team and driving success will make you a valuable team member.

A great teammate gives relentless effort. Give 100%. No one should ever have to tell you to work hard. It is a privilege to be on a team. Never take that for granted. You cannot control many things that will happen during a sports season, but you can control how hard you play. The best way to improve your skills is to give your maximum effort. This pushes your teammates to get better as well. Stay and work after practice and see how many teammates start to join you.

Trust your teammates

Respect others. Recognize that other team members are also trying to fulfill their roles, and consider how you can support them. Take the time to get to know your team. Everyone has a role to play that is no less critical than your own.

Sharing is a principle that is so basic you probably learned it before you were even in school. You should share your time and resources with your team members and, perhaps most importantly, your knowledge and point of view. Great team players think about ways that they can benefit their whole team. Holding back knowledge and resources to benefit yourself is selfish and inconsiderate.

Be prepared

You need to let your team members know that you are dependable. Arriving at work, practice or meetings on time and fully prepared is the best way to show this. It also proves that you are committed to the team.

If you waltz into a meeting 10 minutes late and unprepared, the message you're sending is that your time is more important than the rest of your team's. Be considerate by sticking to schedules and always being prepared.

Accountability

A great teammate holds themselves and their teammates accountable. You should have high standards for yourself and your teammates. If a teammate is not fulfilling duty to the team, you can't be afraid to confront them and get them back on track. You might need to help them buy in to a particular strategy or help them accept their role on the team. Don't accept a negative attitude from teammates, be the player who reaches out to help your team as a whole.

A great teammate takes responsibility. They hold themselves accountable. Your choices, with or away from the team, are a representation of your team, your school or organization, and your family. Everyone associated with your team will be judged by your actions. Is that fair? No. But that's the way it is.

Take responsibility for your behavior and actions at all times. Conduct yourself in a manner that your parents, coaches, and teachers would be proud of. You never know who is looking at you for cues on how to behave.

Know your role (and your limits). Know what's expected of you and how your role fits within the team. Be realistic about how much you can take on. Others depend on you, so make sure you can deliver.

Humility

A great teammate is humble. The player who makes a great play can't wait to pound his chest or call attention to himself is putting himself first. In a team sport, you may be the star of your team or you may have a supporting role. Either way, remember that the team comes first. Your teammates helped give you the opportunity to excel. Put your individual accomplishments aside and acknowledge your teammates. Teams succeed when no one cares who gets the credit.

Your job is to do what it takes to help the team be successful. This isn't always easy, but great teammates find a way to put the success of the team above their own success.

Focus on the team more than the win

Being a member of a successful team is very rewarding, but every member of a winning team has to do his part.

27

On the Shoulders of Giants

"A mentor is someone who sees more talent and ability within you than you see in yourself, and helps bring it out of you." — Bob Proctor

I was not blessed with an abundance of natural athletic skills. I worked hard during the off season and in practice.

I did not play football my sophomore and junior years because of injuries. I injured my knee while snow skiing during the winter of my freshman year. I broke my leg playing baseball the summer between my sophomore and junior years.

I planned to forgo my senior season of football to concentrate on basketball which was my favorite sport. I did not want to jeopardize my basketball season with a possible injury in football. But my football coach wanted me on the team so he recruited me very hard to play my senior season.

During the spring of my junior year, the football coach started suggesting to me that I should go out for football later that fall. He talked about how he needed "Senior Leaders" on the team.

I had never considered myself a leader. I didn't know how to lead!

But he continued to encourage me. He told me how I could make a difference on the team. He made it sound like we would be lucky to win a game without my presence.

Despite the fact that we had an all-state running back on the team and a bunch of other talented athletes, I started to believe that they needed me. He understood young men and what it took to help them succeed.

Coach got me to go out for football. I was the second string quarterback behind a junior returning starter who was fast and athletic. I knew my playing time would be limited to "mop up" unless our starter was injured.

Our quarterback, a far more talented athlete, had a bad knee and the coach knew we could have a good team as long as he had a reliable quarterback. We had an all-state halfback and a great fullback. Coach needed someone to hand it to the running back! He recruited me to be his back up quarterback.

It was almost as if he could see the future because our quarterback injured his knee in the second half of the first game of the season. I came in and handed the ball off as we beat our arch rival in that game. I even intercepted a pass late in the game!

I was the original "game manager" quarterback. As long as I was able to hand it to our star running back without fumbling, we were destined for success. For the most part, I was able to manage the game and we were successful.

We rolled to a number three ranking that year. It was before high school football playoffs in South Dakota so we didn't get to prove ourselves more than that. But it was the most successful football team our school had in more than ten years.

As my confidence grew that season, Coach entrusted me with

throwing the football some. I had a game in which I threw for over 250 yards and three touchdowns, and was named "Ace of the Week" by the regional paper.

None of this happened because I was a special athlete. I listened to my coach, worked hard and focused on the team. I used that football success and confidence to launch my senior basketball season.

Later, my football coach told me he wanted me on the team because I was a good teammate - he thought I could help the team even if I didn't play. He saw something in me that I didn't.

Looking back, Coach knew there was a good chance his quarterback wouldn't make it through the season without injury. He knew he could be successful with a "game manager" playing quarterback. He knew my role in practice during the week was more important than my role during Friday night games.

He saw skills and talents in me I had no idea about. He saw leadership skills in me that could help the team and would serve me well later in life.

Coach Mike Dacy was my first mentor. He was one of the most influential people in my life. I saw him have that same effect on many other young men – sometimes on the football field, sometimes on the basketball court (he was assistant basketball coach as well), and sometimes in the halls of the high school.

Shortly after I graduated from high school, Coach moved on to another nearby school near his wife's home town. I often trade "Coach Dacy stories" with other men who were fortunate enough to come under his tutelage. Each of them was inspired in some way to be a better player, person, or man by him.

Coach Dacy passed away in 2012 at the young age of 65. He was such a great guy. I think of him often. I miss him. I wonder how my life may have been different without his influence. I am lucky to have had him as a mentor.

What is a mentor?

A mentor is a person experienced in a particular field or business who shares the benefits of that experience with a younger person just coming up, sometimes called a mentee.

While that may be a good textbook definition of a mentor, a true mentor is so much more. Having a mentor can provide a range of benefits from practical guidance and role modeling to emotional support and increased self-esteem.

A mentor can provide you with guidance and support as you navigate the challenges of adolescence. This can include advice on school, relationships, career choices, and personal development.

A mentor can serve as a positive role model for you, demonstrating qualities such as responsibility, respect, and perseverance. Seeing these qualities in action can help you develop similar traits and behaviors.

A mentor can help you build self-esteem and confidence by providing positive feedback, encouragement, and constructive criticism.

A mentor can expose you to new ideas, experiences, and opportunities that you may not otherwise encounter. This can broaden your perspective and open up new possibilities for your future.

Adolescence is a challenging and stressful time for young men. A mentor can provide you emotional support and a safe space for you to express your feelings and concerns.

How to Find a Mentor

Look for Role Models - You can start by identifying individuals in your life whom you admire and respect. These can be family members, teachers, coaches, or other adults in the community.

Network - You can also ask for referrals from your family, friends, or other trusted adults. They may be able to connect you with someone who has experience in an area of interest to you. This may be specific (business, attorney, etc.) or it may be qualities you want to exhibit (trustworthiness, reliability, leadership, etc.).

Join Programs or Organizations - Many programs and organizations exist that are specifically designed to match mentors with young people. These include Big Brothers Big Sisters, Boys and Girls Clubs, and scouting organizations.

Seek Out Professionals - If you are interested in a particular career or field, reach out to professionals in that field and ask for advice or mentorship.

It's important that you approach potential mentors respectfully and clearly communicate your goals and interests. It's also important to remember that not every person will be a good fit as a mentor - it may take time to find the right match.

What to Look for in a Mentor

Expertise- The mentor should have expertise in the area you want to learn about or improve in. For example, if you are interested in a specific sport, the mentor should have experience playing or coaching that sport.

Compatibility- You and your mentor should have compatible personalities and communication styles. You should be able to work well together and feel comfortable sharing ideas and feedback.

Reliability- The mentor should be reliable and committed to the mentoring relationship. This means showing up on time, following through on commitments, and being available for regular meetings.

Positive Attitude- The mentor should have a positive attitude and be supportive of your goals and aspirations. They should encourage you to take on new challenges and be willing to offer constructive feedback.

Listening Skills- The mentor should be a good listener and be able to provide guidance and advice that is tailored to your specific needs and interests.

Respectful and Professional - The mentor should be respectful and professional in their interactions with you. They should maintain appropriate boundaries and be mindful of their role as a mentor.

Maybe you have leadership skills you are not aware of. Perhaps you can contribute to a team or organization in ways you don't realize. A good mentor, like Coach Dacy, can help bring those qualities out.

It's important that you trust your instincts and choose a mentor whom you feel comfortable with and can learn from. It may take some time to find the right mentor, but the effort is well worth it in the long run.

28

Count on Me

You may wonder why it is important for you to be reliable. You may know others your age who are not reliable and it doesn't seem to make any difference.

Being reliable allows you to **build trust** with others, including parents, teachers, friends, and future employers. When others can count on a young man to follow through on his commitments and be dependable, they are more likely to trust and respect him.

Reliability is a key component of **responsibility**. By being reliable, you can demonstrate that you are accountable for your actions and that you take commitments seriously. This is an important life skill that will serve you well in the future.

Reliability is often associated with **success**. When you are reliable, you are more likely to achieve your goals and accomplish what you set out to do. This is because reliability shows that you do what you said you would do. This allows you to build a strong reputation, which can lead to more opportunities in the future.

Reliability is also linked to **respect**. When you are reliable, you are showing respect for others by valuing their time and commitments. In turn, others are more likely to show you respect and be reliable in return.

Being reliable can also boost your self-esteem. When you know that you can be counted on to finish the job no matter what, you feel more confident in yourself and your abilities. This can lead to greater happiness and overall well-being.

How do I Become Reliable?

If you agree to do something, you should follow through on it. This could be anything from finishing a school project to helping a friend move.

Arriving on time is an important aspect of reliability. Whether it's showing up for class or meeting a friend, you should make an effort to be on time.

If you are unable to meet a commitment, you should communicate this to the person involved as soon as possible. This shows that you are responsible and respect their time.

If something goes wrong or doesn't go according to plan, you should take responsibility for your actions and do what you can to fix the situation.

Reliability is built over time. You don't go from unreliable to reliable instantly. You need to make an effort to be reliable in all aspects of his life, not just when it's convenient.

Honesty is a key component of reliability. If you are honest with others - and yourself - about what you can and cannot do, you are more likely to be seen as reliable.

Time management is another important skill for reliability. You should make an effort to prioritize your commitments and manage your time effectively to ensure that you can follow through on everything you said you would do.

Being reliable requires effort and consistency. By following through on commitments, being punctual, communicating effectively, being accountable, being consistent, being honest, and practicing good time management, you can build a reputation for reliability and earn the respect of others.

29

One Brick at a Time

"It takes many good deeds to build a good reputation, and only one bad one to lose it." - *Benjamin Franklin*

Tradition is not the worship of ashes, but the preservation of fire.
Gustav Mahler

The Explorers were asked to be the Homecoming parade marshals. While this is exclusively an honorary position, it traditionally goes to a person or couple who is respected for their contributions to the community or school.

The Explorers had made many contributions to the school over the past twenty years, but the current Explorers were relatively new. The eighth graders had two years of service and the seventh graders had a year of service. But the sixth graders had been to three Explorers meetings and were now going to be parade marshalls.

It was time for a visit about tradition and reputation!

Reputation refers to what people think or believe about a person, group, or organization based on their past actions, behavior, and characteristics. It's like the impression that others have of you or your group.

The Explorers had a reputation of service to the community and the school. This was the reason they were asked to serve as parade marshals. Many young men over the prior two decades had worked hard to establish that reputation.

Reputation is fragile. It takes a lot of good work to build it, but just one small mistake or error in judgment can tear it down - for the whole group!

I have often told the group that they will always be remembered as a group for the worst thing any of them does when they are together as a group. Is that fair? No. But it is the way it is.

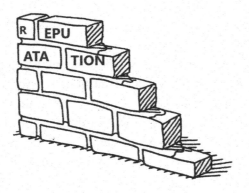

Tradition is a set of customs or practices that a group of people follow because they've been doing them for a long time and consider them important.

The Explorers have a tradition of doing a fall service project.

They hire themselves out to do chores for members of the community in return for a "free will" offering. They pool these funds and give them to someone in the community who is ill or in need of some kind of assistance. This tradition has helped build the group's reputation.

The importance of a group's reputation in the context of tradition can be understood like this:

1. Identity and Unity: Maintaining a positive reputation through traditions helps the Explorers feel more united and connected. When people see that a group consistently follows its traditions, it can create a sense of identity and pride among its members.
2. Respect and Recognition: A good reputation based on positive traditions can earn a group respect and recognition from others. It can make people admire and appreciate the group for their commitment to their customs.
3. Preservation of Heritage: Traditions often reflect a group's cultural or historical heritage. Maintaining a good reputation by upholding these traditions helps preserve that heritage for future generations.
4. Attracting New Members: A group with a positive reputation for meaningful traditions can attract new members who want to be part of something with a strong sense of identity and history.
5. Building Trust: When a group consistently follows its traditions, it can build trust with its members and with the larger community. People know what to expect, which can lead to stronger relationships.

A group's reputation related to their traditions is important because it can help strengthen the group's identity, earn respect, and preserve their cultural heritage, among other things. It's a way for a group to show who they are and what they value.

30

The Balancing Act

"True humility is not thinking less of yourself; it is thinking of yourself less."
— **Rick Warren, The Purpose Driven Life: What on Earth Am I Here for?**

Having the ability to balance confidence with humility is an art. There are very few people who know when to be confident and humble at the right time and in the right measure.

I have lacked confidence most of my life. Humility has always come easier. I have learned to portray confidence (at times), but it does not come easy.

What is Confidence?

Confidence is important because it helps to boost your self-esteem, which is critical during the years when you are going through significant changes in your body and mind. A confident young man is more likely to have a positive self-image and feel good about himself.

Confidence helps you socialize with your peers and form relationships. A confident young man is more likely to participate in class, ask questions, and take academic risks.

Confidence helps build resilience, which makes you better equipped to handle setbacks, rejection, and failure.

How to build confidence

Confidence can be developed over time with intentional effort and practice. Identify your strengths and focus on them. This helps you build a sense of pride and accomplishment, which both help boost your confidence.

Set realistic and achievable goals for yourself, and work towards them (See chapter on *Dream Big (and Write it Down)*). Accomplishing even small goals can give you a sense of accomplishment and confidence. As you achieve more and more goals, your confidence will grow.

Taking care of yourself is crucial to building confidence. Get enough sleep, exercise regularly, eat a healthy diet, and practice good hygiene. Taking care of your physical and mental health can help you feel better about yourself and boost your confidence.

Surround yourself with people who uplift and support you. Seek out positive role models and friends who encourage you to be your best self. Try new things, even if they make you uncomfortable. Stepping outside of your comfort zone can help you grow as a person and build confidence.

Failure is a part of life, and everyone experiences it at some point. Instead of letting failure bring you down, use it as an opportunity to learn. Analyze what went wrong and how you can improve in the future.

What is Humility?

Humility helps you develop emotional intelligence, which is

the ability to recognize and regulate your own emotions and understand the emotions of others. When you are emotionally intelligent, you are more likely to listen and empathize with others, which helps build stronger relationships.

> THERE'S A THIN LINE
> BETWEEN CONFIDENCE
> AND ARROGANCE... ITS
> CALLED HUMILITY.
> CONFIDENCE SMILES.
> ARROGANCE SMIRKS.
>
> Unknown

Humility encourages open-mindedness. Being receptive to new ideas and perspectives leads to better decision-making and problem-solving skills. It allows you to embrace a growth mindset and see mistakes as opportunities to learn, leading to greater academic and personal success as you are more willing to take risks and try new things.

Humility is an important trait for effective leadership as it allows you to lead by example and work collaboratively with others. You are more likely to inspire and motivate you peers by being humble and showing respect for others.

What is Self Awareness?

Self-awareness is the ability to recognize and understand your own thoughts, feelings, and behaviors. It involves being able to reflect on yourself objectively, and assess your own strengths and weaknesses, values, and beliefs. Self-awareness also involves being able to recognize how your actions impact others.

Self-awareness is important because it helps you make better decisions, build stronger relationships, and improve your overall well-being. By understanding your own emotions and behaviors, you can learn to manage your stress, make better choices, and improve your communication skills. Self-awareness can also lead to greater empathy and understanding of others, as you become more attuned to the perspectives and experiences of those around you.

There are several ways to develop self-awareness, including journaling, mindfulness practices, seeking feedback from others, and reflecting on past experiences. By practicing self-awareness, you can gain a better understanding of yourself and your place in the world, which can lead to greater personal and professional success.

Balancing Confidence and Humility

By learning to acknowledge your strengths and accomplishments, but also recognize that you still have room for improvement, you can maintain confidence without becoming arrogant. When you express gratitude for the opportunities and support that have helped you succeed, you can remain humble and recognize that you are not entirely self-made.

If you actively listen to others and show respect for their opinions and perspectives, you will remain humble and open-minded. Then you can take responsibility for your actions and own up to your mistakes, which helps you remain humble and shows you are willing to learn from your experiences.

Setting realistic goals for yourself and working towards achieving them helps maintain confidence without becoming overconfident or complacent.

Overall, achieving a balance between humility and confidence requires a young man to be self-aware, respectful, and willing to learn and grow. By doing so, they can become more effective leaders and build stronger relationships with others.

About the Author

Doug Knust is a passionate advocate for young men. He has spent a lifetime working with and mentoring young men including 20 years with the Explorers Club, 30+ years of teaching religious education to junior high boys and 25+ years of coaching young men.

Knust is a former franchised automobile dealer and small businessman. He holds a BSBA from Creighton University.

Knust loves to hunt, golf, sail and bicycle. He's a political junkie and is interested in all things finance. He has a bourbon collection. He a life long college basketball fan.

He and his wife, Judy, have three grown children and four grandchildren.

You can connect with me on:

- http://manstuffbook.com
- https://twitter.com/ManStuffBook
- https://www.facebook.com/ReadManStuff
- https://www.instagram.com/TheManStuffBook
- http://dougknust.com

Subscribe to my newsletter:

- http://man-stuff.mailchimpsites.com

Also by H. Douglas Knust

Man Stuff: Things a Young Man Needs to Know

Start your young man's journey from boyhood to manhood with Man Stuff! This book will equip him with the confidence and skills necessary to navigate the teenage years with ease. From single mothers to grandparents, this book offers invaluable advice and guidance to help young men make the most of their lives.